Grace & Gratitude

God's Grace | Our Gratitude

Written by
Charnyce Everythings New Perdue
Everythings New Publishing

Grace & Gratitude

Copywrite © 2023 by Charnyce Perdue

All rights reserved. This book may not be reproduced or stored in whole or in part by any means without the written permission of the author except for brief quotations for the purpose of review.

All scripture references have been cited from The Holy Bible, New King James Version (NKJV). 1982, Nelson Bibles by Thomas nelson, Inc. Unless otherwise cited in the text.

ISBN: 979-8-9883405-0-8

Perdue, Charnyce

Edited by Veronica Lee Richardson

Graphics Design by Charnyce Perdue

Everythings New Enterprise Publishing
12495 Limonite Ave., #1096
Eastvale, CA 91752
www.everythingsnew.org

Grace & Gratitude

Table of Contents

How to Use This Devotional 5

Dedication 6

Introduction 9

Grace 19

Gratitude 31

Chapter 1: **Graced to Forgive** 40

Chapter 2: **Grace of Knowing God by Name** 55

Chapter 3: **Graced to Dream!** 66

Chapter 4: **Grace through Grief** 77

Chapter 5: **Graceful Expectations** 85

Chapter 6: **Immeasurable Grace** 98

Chapter 7: **God's Grace Produces:** The Fruits of the Holy Spirit
.... 106

Chapter 8: **Overwhelming to Overjoyed!** 122

Chapter 9: **The Elevation of Gratitude** 136

Chapter 10: **God's Pace of Grace** 148

Chapter 11: **Gracefully Broken** 158

Chapter 12: **A Prayer of Serenity** 176

Chapter 13: **Grace to know You're ENOUGH** 185

Chapter 14: **Faith to Move Mountains** 192

Chapter 15: **Finding Gratitude** 199
Chapter 16: **Guard Your Heart** 210
Chapter 17: **Humiliation vs. Humility** 227
Chapter 18: **Grace and the Soul-Tie Trap** 238
Chapter 19: **A Conversation with Grandma Joyce** 268
Chapter 20: **The Covenant of Grace** 276
Chapter 21: **God's Grace to Pivot!** 287
My List of Gratitude 301
About the Author 313

How to use this devotional

Read each section of this book with an open heart and mind. There is a **Concept, Example, Prayer Application** and **Exercise** in each chapter. As you read, allow the written illustrations to be a gateway to broadening your understanding of your present life and circumstances. Write the Vision of your life for this season in time (Habakkuk 2:2-3). My belief and practice is that "you should only look to your past to see how far you have come", CEVN (Charnyce Everything's New, 2021).

Let God's grace be a path to your gratitude. My prayer is that you will establish a new approach to life and self-awareness. The bible says, in Proverbs 29:18- King Solomon provided sayings of wisdom with instructions and warnings. He said, *"Where there is no vision, the people perish"* (Proverbs 29:18) He went on to say that *"if you are led or have a wise leader, you will be happy in your obedience"*.

Do me a favor, allow God to settle in your spirit through these pages. Challenge yourself to dedicate quiet time to each chapter, so that you can receive the word that God has for you. My hope is that you will get a revelation by the last page of each chapter.

Make yourself a promise that you will take your time, read each passage; and do the work. Don't be apprehensive about reading the book and doing the exercises over and over again. You might be surprised when you're challenged in different ways each time you read through the book. 😊

Dedication

God began giving me the words for this book years before He would tell me it was time to write it. I dedicate this offering of love to my mommy, Sharon Perdue-Harvey. I want to give you your flowers while you're still here.

I honor my maternal grandmother, First Lady Joyce Mitchell. Grandma, your presence lives on through every recollection I have of every conversation we ever had. I say, "See you in heaven", to my Godmother Marlena Brooks. A lady that exuded style and grace in the face of adversity.

I send a shoutout to my Granddaddy Bishop Wilford Mitchell. A man that took his role as a provider as serious as his relationship with Christ. I tell my beloved brother in Christ, Marvin Williams; your presence will forever be with me.

Each person I previously acknowledged are responsible for my growth in God and in meaningful parts of my life. Also, my development as a lady of grace. I am grateful to God for all of you. I Speak Your Name.

Lastly, I dedicate this book to every person that can meet God through the **words He offers through me.** My hope and prayer is that this book will be the catalyst to the next best chapter of your life.

Grace & Gratitude

God's Grace | Our Gratitude

Charnyce Everythings New Perdue

Grace & Gratitude

Introduction

"Dear Heavenly Father. Allow this book to fall in the hands of every person that my message is meant to speak to. I'm honored to share my life and perspective with all the people that you have for me to meet. I thank You in advance for gifting me with every connection this book will make for me.

You are everything to me. I hope that this book is the perfect introduction to those who have yet to meet You. A reminder of Your presence and unmerited favor who are familiar. And a sign of love that will draw Your prodigal children back into close relationship with You. Thank You for this book, and many more to come. In Your name I pray, Amen."

Let me start by saying thank you for purchasing this book. Please do not judge me on how I've chosen to write this book.

On my social media pages, I speak to you like we're having a conversation. I plan to do the same in this book. I don't always speak perfect English.

So, you will notice I often speak and write with slang. Some words will be spelled how they sound in conversation. I even have a few acronyms thrown in here from time to time. Don't worry, I spell them out for you. Don't be alarmed, I'm just being me.

You wanna (want to) know something funny, I started off drafting a book about my life and journey living with lupus.

But God...

The Heavenly Father stopped me dead in my tracks and said,

"I want you to write a devotional."

Now, I can't lie, I was super nervous about diverting from **my** original plan, but I remain obedient. I said a prayer and ask God to write through me, and He did.

I am so… nervous, still! My ball of nerves stem from me not being a minister or theologian (well, at least not yet 😊).

I was afraid that you wouldn't take me seriously without the experience of leading a church, having certification; or license to preach.

Now don't get me wrong, I do have a couple degrees and a few licenses behind my name. However, none of my credentials are in biblical studies or theology, yet 😊 -

But God!!!...

The Holy Spirit calmly whispered to me before my fingers typed the first words,

> *"We got you. God the Father, the Son Jesus Christ; and I, The Holy Spirit. We are here to guide you through writing this book."*

My spirit-girl took a deep breath, smiled, and began to write.

So now, here I am giving you what thus says the Lord! That sounds so official, right!?! I had to slide that in there. I used to hear people say that line all the time in church, lol (laughing out loud) …

No, but for real. I really hope this book speaks to you; the way God has downloaded His message through several life lessons of mine.

Now I know you're probably wondering what this Cali girl could possibly know about speaking to you regarding your life. Well let me say this… I can only speak on what God has brought me through. Not to mention, I can testify to what HE will bring you to. God is my true beginning, middle and end. And I hope that you will develop a relationship one day where you can say the same thing about your relationship with Him, too!

Growing up with a bishop and first lady for grandparents, I should have assumed that one day I would be telling the world about God's goodness and mercy. My grandparents ran and operated their own church. Our family's life revolved around church and work (running different businesses).

There was hardly any room for error, as you could imagine. We ate, breathe, and slept at church. So much so that I thought that everyone in the world had to have had the same upbringing as mine. There couldn't have been any other way. It was:

Jesus Christ + Family + Work + Church

My mom was a choir director, auxiliary leader, and special events coordinator. Those were just some of the roles she played at the church. My mom was also a devoted mother who always put her kids and serving others first. On top of all that, she still made time to make the entire family look like we'd just stepped off the fashion runway every day.

Our family lived our lives either at work or church. Our only day off from church was Thursdays. I guess that was considered our day of rest, lol…

My family was big on Jesus Christ and serving the community. Having such loving and attentive family members, I never really paid attention to the fact that other people I grew up with or went to school with didn't have the foundation of love, guidance, and structure that I had as a child. It would take me years to understand that every parent wasn't like my mommy and her parents.

My granddaddy, who most people referred to as "The Bishop" or "Mr. Willie" was the Provider and Leader. If you came into close contact with him, you wouldn't forget him because he wore this cologne that smelled like money and pizazz. If you attended his church at any time of your life, you were never left unattended.

If the Bishop wasn't checking for you, my grandmother was. That's just how they rolled. And they were good about keeping your secrets or surprises too. They were like speaking your life into a vault. The only way anyone was getting in is if they had the key or code to unlock the door and access the contents of the safe.

My grandma was a beacon of love and understanding. It didn't matter if you were trying to be the super-saint and judge everyone you see. Or, if you were the hoe, prostitute or drug dealer, or gangster on the street. Grandma Joyce or "Big Mama" as so many referred to her; was showing you love.

I'm not even gonna get started on her cooking. My grandma's cooking was straight from heaven. When you ate her food, it's like you ascended into heaven for that period of time.

The savory goodness of Big Mama's cooking was life changing. Now before you ask, no I can't give you a recipe with exact measurements, because she only cooked to taste. I know, I know… I was disappointed too.

It can be hard in these kitchen streets, lol (laugh out loud). But like she always said, if you cook with love, the food will come out right. We'll glean much of her wisdom and love throughout my writings.

My Mommy, Mrs. Sharon- she is everything to me. My Mom exudes poise, strength, faith, diligence and grace all day long! To this day, she's always such a freaking lady (in my Martin Lawrence voice).

I could write an entire book about my mom, but I'll keep it cute for now. My mom has been the ultimate role model for me. Even when she didn't know I was looking; I'd been watching her every move. The way she carries herself. How she pauses before she speaks.

The way she styles her wardrobe. Her tone of voice. Everything about her presence has God's grace dripping all over her.

My mama most definitely has the ***"Grace-Drip"***. When I tell you she's all that and a bag of hot Cheetos; my mom is my "Boo", my "B.A.E" (Before Anyone Else), and she will always be everything to me!

Let me get back to my point. As a child, and even young adult. I looked up to my mom and grandparents. However, They are not the only people that has displayed God's grace for me. Every single interaction I've had in my life has shaped my personality and perception of living and walking with love and grace.

As you read through the chapters, you will read of other people places and experiences that God has shown His amazing grace to me. I hope that you see applied Grace & Gratitude through your reading.

I want to encourage all my creatives out there to do what God instructs you to do. Even if it doesn't make sense. If I can write this book with His guidance and inspiration, you can do what He has for you to do. If writing is your gift, Write the Vision (Habakkuk 2:2-3).

If speaking is your gift. Speak the words that God presents to you. Whatever your gifts are, you can do it! It's true that your gift will make room for you. And if you don't believe me read Proverbs 18:16 NKJV, "A man's gift make room for him and brings him before great men." Proverbs 18:16, NKJV.

This book was written for every person out there who needs pep-talk before you launch into your destiny. Get ready to do your best self-work. That mind, body, and soul work. I hope and pray that this devotional speaks to your heart.

If you happen to be a super-saint and you know words and definitions like the back of your hand, give me a minute to introduce these concepts to those of us who are not so well-versed in scripture.

I'm finding the balance between my gratitude and God's grace for me. God is consistently transforming and renewing me daily. I'm excited to see how God's **"sacred sauce"** called grace changes your name and guides you in peace and direction through this season of Grace & Gratitude.

Let's go and let God show you,

    "What that Grace Do 😊 ."

For the Lord God is a
sun and shield.
The Lord will give
grace and glory.
No good thing will He
withhold
from those who
walk uprightly.

Psalm 84:11, NKJV
Grace

GRACE

Let's start this thang off by defining the word, **Grace**. According to Googles' dictionary, **Grace** is:

"The freely given, unmerited favor and love of God."

The influence or spirit of God operating in humans to regenerate or strengthen them. A virtue or excellence of divine origin. Also called state of **grace**. The condition of being in God's favor or one of the elects" (Google, 2020).

This explanation seems to hit all the major parts of the concept that we'll cover in this devotional. So, we'll roll with this definition as a point of reference. If you believe in a higher power, then you should be familiar with the concept of **Grace**.

God's grace surrounds each and every one of us from the minute we are created in the womb (Psalm 139), to the moment we breathe our last breath.

Grace & Gratitude

My first real example of what grace looks like is my mommy. And, yes, I refer to her as my mommy. As I continue to evolve throughout life, I see God's first true gift of grace over my life. Mrs. Sharon.

You see, my mom was 21 years old when she dissolved the marriage between herself and my bio-dad. She once told me that if she didn't leave the relationship, somebody was going to hell, and the other was going to jail. Her words, not mine 😊.

However, by the grace of God, she didn't have to go either of those routes. My mom had the wisdom and fortitude to call on her village to help her reestablish herself as a single mother and get on her feet. She had 3 toddlers, with one on the way.

It was several years before this dream of hers would become her reality. Now I don't know about you, but I could shout right now! When I think of the goodness of God and how He brought my mommy through such a trying transition in her life, I know for sure He is real!! (Praise hands raise).

Let me calm down before I start shouting and get off track, lol… I just see God's grace all over that thang! I'm not sure if I could have done all of what she did at such a young age. Or even today if I'm being 1000!

As I grow older and observed how my mom moves through life, I see what walking in grace looks like. My mom never spoke ill of my dad when I was young and inquiring about their marriage. Or asking questions to learn about my father.

My mom whole life screams grace. My silly nickname for her is "Mary the mother of Jesus", lol… I call her that because she is so innocent in nature. She's not a woman that desires to party, drink, smoke, deceive or control others. She just wants to serve God, love, and cover her family, work hard, and retire well.

Now, don't get me wrong; I'm sure she can tell you off if you cross the line with one of her kids. But for the most part she's one of the sweetest women I've ever known. That sweet nature just exemplifies grace for me.

My foundation of grace outside of my residential home was pretty solid as well. You see, I grew up in church. My grandparents own and operated the church.

I guess you can say that I come from a 1st family. Now granted, my family had a small church, however it was a church, nonetheless. I say small because their church housed about 250 people. You know these days churches normally seat 500+ people. However, whether the building held 250 occupants or not, that place was bursting at the seams with people ready to praise the name of Jesus.

You see, I come from a nondenominational Christian background. However, my grandparents were brought up in the Church of God in Christ denomination. Once my grandfather got saved and wanted to start a church, he said that he didn't want to categorize his church by any specific denomination because anyone who loved God and wanted to worship at the church was welcomed.

Growing up in church I heard people say things like, "By God's grace I am here." Or "When I think of the goodness of Jesus and all He's done for me; my soul cries out hallelujah! Thank God for saving me." Then the person would burst out with a shout, some crazy foot work, or even a loud praise to God.

I wasn't sure what that was all about until my twenties. It just seemed like someone who wanted attention during praise and worship, or the testimony portion of church service.

Then one day in my early twenties I had an encounter with God that changed the course of my relationship with Him. I was enjoying praise and worship and the lyrics from the song pierced my heart. It wasn't so much the words of the song as it was the atmosphere in the room. God met me right where I was.

The Holy Spirit started speaking to me about different people in my life that I needed to show grace towards.

Tears fell on my cheeks, and I just remember saying,

"Whatever You want me to say, I'll say. Whatever You want me to do, I'll do."

I would learn years later that God was preparing my heart. He was preparing me to activate His magnificent **Grace**. God began to teach me lessons in how to walk, talk, and react with **Grace**. How to respond with a heart of understanding and empathy. How to place His love on everything and anyone that I encountered.

God has shown me that there will be times in your life where you can be reactive to your circumstances, or reliant on His Holy Spirit to guide you. Allowing God to move on your behalf by trusting and following Him, as He orders your steps.

It's my belief that that's exactly what my mom did when she made the tough decision to end her marriage and choose a different course of life for herself and her children.

When life events have you staring down a dark road, how do you cope? Do you trust God and ask the Holy Spirit to be a lamp to your feet and light your path? (Psalm 119:105-112). Or do you choose to allow your current circumstances to get the best of you; and wallow in the blame-game and indecision?

As for me, I choose God!!! My mom's relationship with God guided her through her tough times and helped her see the light of her future during so much darkness. I am certain that HE will do the same for you and me 😘.

Have you ever been in a dark place in life and didn't know what to do? Well, I have a suggestion, Try God! The bible tells us in 2 Corinthians 12:9, that God's grace is enough for whatever circumstance we're facing. His power is made strong in our weakness. So, with God's word being true, if you give Him your problems, **He Will Not Fail You!** And that's point blank **periodt!** Yes, I said **"periodt"** with a "t," lol…

I believe in the Heavenly Father's act of Grace so-much-so, that I will be sharing several different instances where He has been here for me, time and time again. Now, I'm not gonna lie; it took living my life out and communing with God to know that He's got my back.

Matter of fact, He got my back, front, both sides, top and bottom. However, it took me a while to fully trust Him. I had to let go of what people would think of me when I started walking solely by my faith in Father God.

Doing my research, I came across phrases like the Dispensations of grace, the Law of Grace; and lastly, the difference between Grace and Mercy. But what had happened was… I didn't want to dive too deep into the topic of grace and loose those new to the concept. So, I checked with the Holy Ghost and God let me know that it was okay to save the more in-depth concepts for Grace & Gratitude volume 2 or 3.

Yes, yes; this thang gets even deeper before it even begins. Follow me on social media for more information on upcoming projects (wink, wink!... 😊).

Besides, my desire is that we take small bites of such a good topic as **Grace**. I want to make sure we digest this meal correctly. My grandma would say, "eat the meat, throw away the bones."

In the bible the scripture says that babes becoming acquainted with the word of God were feed milk before meat (1 Corinthians 3:2; 1 Peter 2:2; Hebrews 5:12). Just to name a few.

So, this first installment of God's **Grace** be "milk." Seeing that I'm a foodie of sorts, I can appreciate working my way from appetizer to entree. I want to savor each and every morsel in this meal of **Grace**.

Since God is teaching us both, I want to make sure we get this word and we're able to truly understand what's been gifted to us. Needless to say, we are in this thang together (wink, wink … 😊).

Prayer

Dear Heavenly Father. Thank you for giving me the insight to purchase and read this devotional. Help me to grow in the ways that You see fit. Let the words of my mouth (and pen), and the meditation of my heart be pleasing and acceptable to You oh God. In Your mighty name I pray, Amen.

Exercise

Your first task for this devotion will be to write down what grace means to you. Don't worry about anyone reading your answers. This journey is between you and God. Just write what first comes to mind. Now let's get this thang crackin'.

Grace & Gratitude

Write It Down ...

Rejoice always.
Pray without ceasing.
In everything
give thanks;
for this is
the will of God
in Christ Jesus for
you.

1 Thessalonians 5:16-18
Gratitude

GRATITUDE

Before we jump right into the Gratitude of it all. Let me just let you know that I will call Gratitude by a few names:

Gratitude, Thanks, Thankfulness, Appreciation

Basically, I don't want you to be thrown off by the changing of the word. I will be using these words interchangeably.

When I originally thought of the word or act of Gratitude, I said to myself;

> "Hey! I'm grateful for everything and everyone in my life.

Then I had to take a step back and be for real with myself. The Holy Ghost already knew the real deal deep down in my corazón, lol 😉 .

Now, I haven't always been, nor have I consistently displayed sentiments of thankfulness in my life. Especially not as a child or young adult.

Matter of fact if I'm being super real with you; it took me a cool minute (i.e., years….) to apply gratitude to my everyday agenda.

When I woke up and before I fell asleep, I would pray for my family and friends. Pray for my health and strength. Then I would briefly acknowledge God for His presence in my life. However, there was no,

> "My Father which art in heaven, hallowed be Thy name."

Not nan-nother time did I give God thanks in any sense of the word for just being who He is to me. And if you ever have to wonder; HE (God) is **everything** to me.

The air I breathe when I wake up in the morning. The Praise, Worship, R&B and Trap Music that my heart sings daily. And yes, I did say R&B and Trap music. My God is a lover and a gangster, like that. The reason for me even writing these words to you.

He's all that and then some.

With me stating that God is all that to me, I had to really revisit the art and practice of Gratitude. What is it really?

So, I went to the dictionary to see what that definition was talking about. Then I followed up with scripture to solidify and cross reference my findings. Let's break this thang down. According to Google, Gratitude is defined as:

> Gratitude (/ˈgradəˌt(y)o͞od/); noun
> the quality of being thankful; readiness to show appreciation for and to return kindness.
>
> Example:
> "She expressed her gratitude to the committee for their support."

That's easily understood, right? Then you type in:

> "How is **Gratitude** defined in the bible?", and you get scriptures like:

1. 1 Thessalonians 5:18
2. Psalm 118:24
3. Colossians 3:15
4. Psalm 107:1
5. Matthew 6:2

In this devotional book you will find many scripture references throughout this book pertaining to Gratitude. With each passage speaking on giving thanks, you will see that I have used the New King James Version of the bible as a main source.

Me coming from a church all-day-everyday background, I often think of scriptures like "Oh give thanks unto the Lord, for He is worthy to be praised"(Psalm 106:1; NKJV).

That scripture has been made into praise and worship songs throughout the years, so the words and melody easily comes to mind when I think of giving thanks for anything in life.

Anyone who's ever attended an African American church in North America that has a little bit of pep in their music department can attest to clapping their hands and stomping their feet to this song. I've never been to a church that didn't sing it, lol…

With me doing all that clapping, stomping, and waving my hands; I still didn't directly connect to my mindset of gratitude in relation to God. I just sang the songs, paid my tithes and offering, and left with that song in my heart.

But, come Sunday night or Monday morning I was back to worrying about whatever life would throw my way; than thanking and praising God in advance for what He would bring me through. And Him being all that He is to me.

Then I stop and begin to wonder, if you didn't grow up in church like me, where you heard songs and scriptures reciting these words continuously; how do you connect with the word; **Gratitude**? Would the word mean the same to you as it does to me?

Maybe… Possibly not. So, I asked God to help me share some relatable experiences I've had over the years with you, that will paint a clearer picture for you. I'm not one of those, "so heavenly bound, that I'm no earthly good", type of people. I'm sure you'll figure that out as we move throughout the text.

Back to Gratitude… As I continued my search of examples in the bible of thanks; I didn't find the word gratitude. I wondered why God gave me that word for this book title, instead of Thankfulness. Here's why.

There's the **"act"** of thankfulness; then a **"mindset"** of gratitude. When God gave the revelation, it blew my perfectly sculped baby-hair back! Lightbulb moment! Even better, God-Moment!

You see, when your heart is open to follow God's word and design for your life, you not only speak a word of thanks, but you LIVE a life of Gratitude. You give thanks in everything that transpires in your life.

Be it large or small. Whether others can see your transformation. Or even if it's only a precious moment between you and God. For that reason alone, we will learn to practice and apply Gratitude throughout this book. We will set our minds and hearts on things above. Just like the scripture says in Colossians 3:2-10 (NKJV).

Prayer

Dear Heavenly Father. I come to you, open, ready, and willing to learn how to activate my gift of thanks and praise. Help me to develop my application and appreciation for who You are in my life. Open my heart and mind as I begin to see Your will for me. Allow me to see me the way You see me. In Your mighty name I pray. Amen.

Exercise

Let's put this thang into practice. Jot down a few lines about your relationship with God. What does a relationship with Him look like to you? Do you find yourself giving Him thanks for your life? How do you see your relationship with Him developing from here on out?

Write it Down!

And the child grew and became strong in spirit, filled with wisdom, and the grace of God was upon Him.

Luke 2:40, NKJV
Grace

Chapter 1
Graced to Forgive

I think it's best to start this journey of grace off with the act of **Forgiveness**. You're probably asking yourself, "why would she start this book off with such a serious topic?"

Let me tell you. It's my belief that you cannot grow and move forward in life unless you employ the act of *forgiveness*. Also, the enemy, Satan will trap you in a mental and emotional mindset of bondage with unforgiveness. Which turns into holding grudges and even hating others, or more importantly; hating or punishing yourself. But my Father God and my main-man Jesus Christ; have a way of turning the enemies' plot of destruction and confusion around to bless you.

Let's start with the definition of forgiveness. According the psychologytoday.com,

Forgiveness is defined as, "the release of resentment or anger."
 The research goes on to state that the action to forgive is to,

"stop feeling angry or resentful toward (someone) for an offense, flaw, or mistake."

We will use these definitions for reference, along with a few scripture references to make this concept concrete for us.

While in college, in order to advance in any counseling or therapeutic profession, a person must be proficient in conducting therapy. Therefore, the student must first attend therapy themselves.

I know you're probably saying, "girl, what does therapy have to do with forgiveness and God's grace?" Be patient, I'm gonna break it all down to a low gravy, as my grandma use to say 😊 .

In therapy there was a saying that was told to me that I now share with my clients,

"Forgiveness is for you, not the person that hurt you".

I am also sure to mention that when you are applying forgiveness to others, make sure you save some grace and forgiveness for yourself. I've always considered myself to be a fairly open-hearted and understanding person, but I too had to deal with unforgiveness in my family life. Like to hear it, here it goes.

The concept of forgiveness was present at a very early age for me. I know I stated in the introduction pages that I grew up surrounded by love and protection in my upbringing. However, there was a very large missing piece to my hearts' puzzle from the womb. You see I was born during a turbulent time in my mom's life. My parents married and started a family incredibly young.

My mom was eighteen and my dad was twenty. Now, for whatever reasons they married so young, I don't have the details. However, 4 years, 3 babies, and one in the womb later; the two young adults were now divorcing. I just happened to be the baby in mom's belly when she divorced my dad.

Growing up, I spent most of my time with my mom and her parents. Due to my family's life being busy with running a church and being entrepreneurs, there was little time to ponder on where my dad was. As I grew older, I began to notice that I wasn't going on the weekend visits to daddy's house.

When my dad would come pick up my older three siblings, I first wondered why my daddy would always say,

> "I'll take you next time."

As the years rolled by, I felt my heart growing further away from my dad. I stopped paying attention to the calendar.

I no longer checked to see if it was his weekend to pick "us" up, because I wasn't going anyway. So, what was the point of worrying about if it was his weekend or not.

What I didn't realize then is that, because I didn't spend any physical time with my father, I developed no emotional attachment to him. With there being no emotional attachment, a disregard for his presence in my life started to grow.

That small seed of disregard grew into dismissiveness and later disrespect and bitterness towards my dad.

All along, I thought I was doing great. I figured it was okay that I didn't have a relationship with my biological father because I had my mom and my grandparents. But the years to come would prove otherwise. My mom and my bonus-dad (stepdad) married when I was about twelve years old and now there was a man in the house.

Now granted, I have an awesome relationship with my bonus-dad; however, I didn't know how him having entered the home would shift my thinking and heart posture about having a father in my life. Seeing how caring and loving my stepdad was with my mom and their combined total of 9 kids was amazing.

When he brought snacks home, he brought snacks for everyone. The icing on the cake was that my bonus-dad was the same with his other children as he was with his bonus kids.

Sometimes I would ride with him to take things over to his ex-wife, and their children. He would buy double the number of snacks or food. There was no difference in the treatment of one set of children than the other.

While my love and respect grew for my stepdad, resentment festered for my bio-dad. At the age of eighteen I remember finding an envelope with my bio-dad's address on it. I dressed the envelope and placed it on my desk in my room. I then sat on my bed and wrote my daddy a letter expressing how I felt about not having him in my life.

If I could take the words back today, I would. Even though I was in emotional pain, I could have expressed my hurt and disappointment of our lack of relationship in a much more respectful and gracious way than I did.

In so many words I told him that I was a successful young adult without any help from him. That was rude and uncalled for.

You see, just because you have a bad experience with someone, it doesn't give you the right to hurt them in return. The bible says if you want friends, you must first show yourself friendly (Proverbs 18:24).

I wouldn't put forgiveness into practice with my bio-dad until many years down the line. However, God had already started laying the framework for the olive branch that I would grow for my biological father, by placing my stepdad in my life.

After high school, I attended Cal State University San Bernardino. While majoring in psychology, I learned about the human mind and emotions. One day my psychology professor presented the attachment theory.

The professor went on to explain that your mind and emotions are responses to your psychological attachments. I immediately thought to myself, "here goes those thoughts about my daddy again".

The term reminded me of my lack of relationship with my bio-dad. And when I calculated my last real communication with my dad, it had been four years that passed.

What I realized was, my lack of emotional attachment to my daddy was still ever-present in my life. That letter that I wrote him at 18 years old wasn't gonna cut it. Neither would it balance out the unresolved feelings I had towards him. I would need to mend the broken chain-linked fence between the two of us.

Now don't think that this thought didn't come without some serious back-and-forth with my spirit and the Holy Spirit. At first, I was all in my feelings. I remember me and my boyfriend at the time was taking that psychology class together.

One day my boyfriend and I were hanging out and I asked him about his relationship with his dad. He told me that much like me, he really only had a connection with his mom. Then he asked me about my relationship with my biological father.

My boyfriend had already met my step-dad, so I couldn't lie and say my bio-dad didn't exist. Before I could speak any negative words about my dad, I simply told my boyfriend that my dad wasn't really that active in my life; and that I didn't have the desire to interact with him.

My boyfriend could sense the anger and dismissive tone in my voice. That anger was really unprocessed pain. We hugged with a moment of silence. He could tell that talking about my dad was a touchy subject. We left the subject of my dad alone that day. But the Holy Spirit would have me revisit those emotions later.

While in a class lecture a God-moment hit me. Both my boyfriend and I were sitting in class, and the professor presented the lesson of The *Power of Forgiveness*. The professor stated that forgiveness is not for the person that has harmed you. Forgiveness is for you. The concept hit me like a ton of bricks.

How could forgiving my dad help me?

I wasn't the parent, **he was**

I wasn't the one making empty promises, **he was** 😔 ....

I wasn't the one missing all the important life-moments, **he was** 🥱 -

I didn't dare look at my boyfriend during the lecture, because I knew we had just had this conversation the other day. After class, he held my hand, and I told him about my God-encounter. I said, "I think it's time I really forgive my dad".

We made eye contact and smiled at each other and went on to the next class. I had made-up in my mind that I would commit to getting to know my dad and loving him for just being my dad.

Life continued and still no real relationship had been established between my dad and me. Now it's 2011, and I am attending graduate school and the concept of *forgiveness* presented itself, yet again.

My God-moment arrived like a blaring flashing light. All I could hear God say was,

"You need to forgive him".

I knew exactly who the Holy Spirit was referring to. I thought I'd addressed the issue on my end, but I guess not. I hadn't had a conversation with my dad.

I wasn't calling or checking up on him with any regularity. So how could I have truly forgiven him? Then the Holy Spirit repeated the scripture, *"If you want friends, you must show yourself friendly"* (Proverbs 18:24, NKJV). Seeing that this scripture is based in the book of wisdom, I had to take note; then act on it.

I didn't know how I would approach my daddy, so I just called and left a message for him to call me back. Some time had passed before he returned my call. While waiting on my daddy's response, God began to work on my heart posture. What I learned was, I can't control how people treat me. I'm only in control of how I respond to their treatment.

So, I made-up in my mind that I would love my dad for being my dad. And I would show him the love and respect that I wanted to receive from him. That's something that I'd learned from my mom.

Grace & Gratitude

My dad and I have a better relationship today, and I have God to thank for that. We speak often and we're constantly learning about one another. Had I not forgiven my dad and extended the olive branch of communication, there's no telling whether we would have a relationship today or not.

When I opened my heart and mind to forgive my dad, I was set free. At that moment I was able to begin a new relationship with my dad and receive closure from my past. Sometimes it's as simple as showing yourself friendly.

God's grace is shown through the act of forgiveness. So be bold in your efforts to forgive. And if the grievance you have is with yourself, lay that pain at God's feet. He will guide you through forgiving yourself.

Prayer

Let's Pray. Dear Heavenly Father, I come to You in need of strength and transparency. Lord, please help me to open my understanding of Forgiveness. Help me to apply this practice to myself as well as to others. Help me to be open and honest about my true emotions for the things that have happened in my life. Help me to forgive myself and others who I know, and feel, have harmed me. Because all things work together for the good of those who love You (Romans 8:28).

I now know that applying the act of forgiveness will bless me and free me of past and present hurt. Thank You for this word. In Your name I pray, Amen.

Exercise

Take some time to think about the people in your life who might need an olive branch from you. Write their names down. If you need to forgive yourself, write your name down as well.

Whether you speak to them or not, take a moment and think about if you feel comfortable communicating with them. If you can, give them a call or shoot them a text message. If they've gone on to be with the Lord, simply speak their name aloud and let them know you are thinking of them. Remember,

Forgiveness *is not for them; it's for* **you** 🥹. Ting!

Write Your Heart Out

Grace & Gratitude

Bless the Lord, Oh my soul
And forget not all His benefits.
Who forgives all you iniquities,
Who heals all your diseases
Who redeems your life
from destruction,
Who crowns you with lovingkindness
And tender mercies,
Who satisfies your mouth
with good things,
So that your youth is renewed
like the eagles.

Psalm 103:2-5
Gratitude

Chapter 2

The Grace of Knowing God by Name

Growing up in church, certain things I didn't recognize was a real plus when evolving in life. I would always hear the older saints and church members telling their testimonies and referring to God by different names. I didn't understand the power that resound in God's names.

As I grew older and started taking more of an interest in deepening my relationship with God, I took it upon myself to research the different names of God. So now I will share His name with you.

God's Names & Descriptions:

Elohim - God, My Creator
El Shaddai - God Almighty
El Elyon - Most High God
El Olam - God Everlasting, God Eternal
El Roi - God Who Sees
Adonai - Lord, Master
Yahweh - God
Jehovah Jireh- Lord Provided (Provider)
Jehovah Nissi - God, My Banner
Jehovah Sabaoth - The Lord of Hosts
Jehovah Mekeddeshem- The Lord Who Sanctifies me
Jehovah Shalom - The Lord Our Peace
Jehovah Shammah - The is There
Jehovah Tsidkednu- The Lord Our Righteousness

My Story

Before the era of The Affordable Healthcare Act of 2011; or what most like to refer to as, Obama Care. Life was hard for those of us who were living with a preexisting illness. I was in desperate need of health insurance. The year was 2007, and I was struggling within my body. I remember it like it were yesterday.

I was amid a lupus flare and visiting the nearest county hospital for doctor visits and medication. I had recently returned from living in Atlanta Georgia, for 6 months. I was jacked up y'all. I was too sick to get a job, and too physically weak to even fake it until I made it.

The lupus symptoms were rearing their ugly heads, one after the other. I was losing my hair; my energy was non-existent, and I was starting to develop heart problems.

The county physician that was handling my case read my lab test results and was grieved. He then told me,

> "Ms. Perdue, you need to find a way to get some health insurance benefits. I've taken your treatment as far as I can go at this facility. You need to be treated by medical specialists before it's too late."

What he didn't want to tell me was that my heart tissues and muscles were so weak that I was in danger of having a heart attack or stroke. He then told me I had atrial fibrillation, and that I needed to see a cardiologist as soon as possible.

The doctor suggested that I go to the County Social Services office to see if I could apply for Medicare. He informed me that if I were able to receive Medicare, then I would be able to see medical specialists who specialized in autoimmune diseases and the appropriate treatments for possible organ failure.

I went to the county office trying to request support services because I was tore up from the floor up. But I guess I didn't look sick. I made the mistake of combing my hair and putting on a little makeup to cover the "butterfly rash" that displayed the lupus flare on my face. That was the wrong thing to do.

When I sat down with the county worker, she briefly looked over my paperwork. The doctor asked if I had children and a place to live. She then printed out a receipt for the application and paperwork I submitted and informed me that the county would mail me their response.

Weeks went by before I received correspondence from the county office. The department had denied my request to receive medical services.

By this point I was so weak I couldn't take myself back to the county office to submit my appeal. So, my mom took me down to the office to submit my appeal paperwork. By this time, I was in a wheelchair. The front of my head was balding from stress and medication. And the remaining hair looked like strands of cat fur.

Jehovah Rapha …

The front desk attendant directed me and my mom to an older county worker who could tell I was in despair. I had no energy to comb my hair or cover the butterfly rash with makeup this time. Anyone who was paying attention could see that I was desperate for help. My spirit was broken, and my body was exhausted.

Jehovah Jireh…

This woman must have been a guardian angel because she immediately started to give my mom and I the information we needed to qualify for healthcare and financial assistance.

She asked me a few questions, wrote down a number and address to the Social Security Administration office and placed a call to make me an appointment to meet with someone that week.

After my mom and I gathered our things to leave her desk, the worker gently touched my hand and said,

"God bless you sweetie."

I felt the grace of the Holy Spirit in her embrace. I said thank you and we left the office.

El Olam...

It had to be the spirit of the Lord that pricked that woman's heart to help me and my mom that day. She literally wrote down, step-by-step; what to do. The worker wrote down which department to call first and the information that we needed to provide for each call. **That was God!**

I thank God every day for meeting that doctor who directed me to apply for Medicare. And I am also grateful for that older county worker that wrote the offices and process down in detail for us.

What I learned through that experience was that God is always with you no matter what situation you find yourself in. I recall the look of despair and being overwhelmed on my mother's face. However, she was determined to help me get well. My body was weak, but my spirit was strong.

During this time in my life, I was barely learning God's names and meanings. But let me tell you this, when I started calling God by his names in my prayer time, it seemed like He was right there in the room with me. I was no longer alone.

The Holy Spirit filled my broken spirit with the peace of **Jehovah Shalom**. When I needed services and resources, He was right there to provide as **Jehovah Jireh**.

When I offered up a heart of thanks, the process became easier. I stopped getting the "run around" treatment from the different governmental agencies. If you've ever needed assistance, you know exactly what I'm talking about. I received the help that I needed. And it was quick, fast, and right on time.

Grace & Gratitude

I've experienced so many times in my life where my circumstances left me speechless. Some experiences were good times. Other times, not so great. You know those times when your back is against the wall, and you can't tell your left side from your right. We all have situations where you've needed help, and no one can help you. Not even your loved ones. Where your troubles were even outside of your support system's ability to assist you. That's when you learn to call God by name.

I will encourage you to start addressing the Heavenly Father by name after reading this chapter. I'm sure there's a situation or circumstance that you can pick one or maybe all the names from the "God name list", and use it right now 😉

Prayer

Dear Heavenly Father, I would like to thank you for introducing me to your many identities. Please help me to identify how I can connect to you by calling you by name. Point out the various situations in my life and the name to call so that I can see your grace. I appreciate your presence, direction, and guidance. In your name I pray, Amen.

Exercise

What do you think would happen if you addressed God by HIS name. Maybe you could receive clarity, direction, purpose. Or even resources like me.

Why don't you try it for yourself. Write down your current situation or circumstance(s).

Place the name of God next to the circumstance. If you dare to take it a bit further, google a bible verse that matches the keyword in your situation.

Place that scripture on a sticky note and commit it to God in prayer.

When God starts to answer your prayers, do me a favor- Shoot me an email, DM or text message. I can't wait to hear and read how calling Him by name works out for you. ❤️

Grace & Gratitude

Write to His Name

Grow in the
grace and knowledge
of our Lord and
Savior Jesus Christ.
To Him the glory,
both now
and forever.
Amen.

2 Peter 3:8, NKJV
Grace

Chapter 3

The Grace to Dream!

"God is the author and finisher of our faith," (Hebrews 12:2). What if I told you that you are God's Dream. Would you believe me? It's my belief that God had a hope and a future for you, long before He created you (Psalm 139). If you are God's vision, what makes you think He wouldn't give you a vision? He says in Jeremiah 29:11, "He knows the thoughts and plan that He has for you. To prosper you. So why not take His word for it.

There's a couple of things that I've come to realize about the Heavenly Father. He gifts you with free choice and the ability to Dream! Inside of you is where endless possibilities and awaiting materialized visions reside.

Do you doubt that God will do the impossible for you? If so, God says, " *try Me and see*", (Malachi 3:10).

Soon you will be quoting Philippians 4:11-13; "I can do all things through Christ that strengthens me." But first you will have to believe it.

I have been testing out this dream theory in my own life for some time now. When I tell you the Lord comes through for me, HE comes through. The dreams He shows me; I write them down. Matter of fact, the Holy Spirit commanded me to write the vision (Habakkuk 2:2-3) in my early twenties.

I began placing His word (scripture) on each dream or idea, and I placed them on my vision board or in my journal. Seeing that I am in recovery for procrastination; I jump to it, knowing that if I wait too long; I may lose the vision or forget what He's shown me.

Let's take for instance my first vision board that I created in 2009. I was fresh off recovering from a horrific lupus flare that almost took me out! I'd lost the peripheral vision in my right-eye due to a stroke. I was also recovering from a heart attack and pneumonia, at the same dang time.

I had to learn how to walk and talk again. My cognitive association was off for weeks; but I could see God's plan for me. My body was in such disarray that my team of medical doctors ordered that I take high dosages of several different medications that would pretty much keep me asleep, while my body started to heal.

During my heavily medicated sleeps, HE (God) would show me why He spared my life. I saw school, marriage, family, business opportunities; and so much more.

I don't know about y'all, but most often when you dream good dreams, you're unable to remember the dream. Or at least not in detail. Well during this particular recovery period, I was seeing these visions in what felt like "real time". I could feel these dreams at my fingertips.

So, I went to God and ask Him to help me put the dreams down on paper. I grabbed some magazines and began cutting out pictures that matched the vision that God revealed to me. Once I had all the pictures posted on my board, God gave me scriptures to confirm his word for me. I had things like:

Graduate school

Author

Administrator

Marriage

Rest & Relaxation

Motherhood, etc....

Not one of the things listed above was my reality in 2008. I was barely getting back to walking, talking, and starting to feed myself. If you can believe it, my muscles were so weak from the pneumonia coursing through my body that I didn't possess enough strength to put a fork or spoon in my mouth.

But I believed God-

It's like HE read the inscription on the walls of my heart, and I felt a sense of supernatural strength begin to build up inside me. As I to regain my strength, I asked my parents to sit my laptop on my lap and bring me a bible.

I then started researching graduate school options. My mentors encouraged me to do the research and visit the schools that spoke to my spirit. So, I did just that. I didn't know how I would pay for school or if I had what it took to be accepted to my school of choice, but God knew.

By 2010 I'd done the groundwork and narrowed my choices down to Azusa Pacific and Loma Linda University. I toured Azusa first, and the school was beautiful, but my desired program was compacted and would require me to stretch beyond my current physical and financial capabilities. That option would most likely become a stressor for me. So, Azusa was off the table.

Two days later I had an interview at Loma Linda University. When I drove up on the campus, the atmosphere shifted. It felt like home. I went in to take the tour and one of the department professors from the school of Social Behavioral Sciences that was in his office wanted to speak with me.

I was kind of caught off guard because I wasn't prepared for an interview. He asked me if I knew exactly what I was majoring in and I told him, "I'm majoring in People. I then said I want to help people like so many who have helped me.

I wanted to provide therapeutic guidance and help them find resources for self-sufficiency." He smiled, wrote my name down; we shook hands, and he took me straight to the admin office to speak with Dr. Mary Moline.

Mrs. Moline is a psychologist, published author and professor. We had a brief conversation of what led me to consider LMU and she smiled and said,

> "I think this university would be a good fit for you".

She handed me an example of a course syllabus and an application for admission. She wrote down the name of a person that I should speak with in the financial aid department, and the rest is history.

I entered graduate school at Loma Linda University in Winter 2010 and God carried me through. I received the funding I needed to complete the program. Met and worked with some of the greatest minds in the fields of therapy and social work. And all because I followed God's lead and dared to **DREAM**.

I trusted God's word and plans for my life even when I was coming fresh off my death bed. And guess what, HE turned my dreams into reality. Everything that I placed on my vision board has manifested thus far. I'm so geeked (excited) because I have expanded my original board and placed new goals and visions that HE has shown me on the board.

The God-moment I had by feeling the sense of home when I drove up on the campus of Loma Linda University was the Holy Spirit confirming that LLU was the university for me. Then the Heavenly Father doubled down with the confirmation by me, bumping into the 1st professor that would lead me to the office of Dr. Mary Moline.

Let me say this, I did not have to take the GRE, and I actually didn't have the GPA to qualify for admissions to the university, but God still made my dreams do what they did 😊.

My courage + God's grace= Me speaking to you through this book. Are you starting to see those dreams yet? I can't wait to see them come to pass for you! Now it's your turn to chart God's vision for your life.

Prayer

Dear Heavenly Father reveal Your word and plan to me, oh God. Help me to write the Vision that you have for my life (Habakkuk 2:2-3). I thank You in advance for the future manifestation of my dreams. I believe that Your will is to make my dreams a reality. Give me the patience I need to wait on You (Psalm 27:14). I believe that Your word will come to past. In your name I pray. Amen.

Exercise

Okay you may need those sticky notes now! Write down all the dreams/visions God has given you. Then google key words to see if there is a scripture attached to those words or phrases. Write it all down. Then pray and watch God turn your dreams into reality!

Grace & Gratitude

Write Your Dreams!

12 I have learned both to be full and to be hungry, both to be abound and to suffer need.
13 I can do all things through Christ who strengthens me.

Philippians 4:12-13
Gratitude

Chapter 4
Graced through Grief

I love watching movies and tv series in my spare time. My favorite genres are romantic comedies, fantasy, and stories based on true life events. Recently, I watched the movie "The Immortal Life of Henrietta Lacks". The movie was a true story about Mrs. Henrietta Lacks, a black woman whose cells were harvested by doctor's and used to cure many different diseases in modern day medicine. Mrs. Henrietta's cells are still being used to this day. Amazing, right?!

Well, the trickery of it all was Mrs. Henrietta didn't volunteer her cells. She was deceived by doctors and told that she had one diagnosis while being experimented on, to find treatment and cures for other diseases. I don't want to give away the entire movie.

So, I'll just say you should check this movie out immediately. For the sake of this chapter, I'll try to highlight a situation that stood out to me without giving away too much of the storyline.

In one particular part of the movie, one of Henrietta's children, Deborah was obsessed with knowing the truth about her mother's case and how she died.

While working with journalist who was covering the case, Deborah learned that one of her siblings, her sister was abused in a mental facility; and the sister died while in the care of the mental institution.

After learning of her sisters abuse and death, Deborah suffered an emotional breakdown. She raced over to her uncle's house to tell him about the research and medical records findings she'd uncovered from the medical institution.

Deborah placed herself in her sister's shoes, the pain from the truth she learned about her sister's life in the institution tore her apart. With her emotions running all over the place, Deborah became grief-stricken.

Her uncle realized that his niece was in the midst of a manic episode, so he grabbed Deborah and held her in his arms. After asking God to take the burden of memories from his niece. He began to sing,

> "Welcome... into this place.
> Welcome... into this broken vessel.
> You desire to abide in the praises of Your people.
> So, we lift our hands....
> As we lift our hearts....
> And we offer up this praise unto Your Name."

The uncle rocked his niece back and forth in his arms. He told Deborah that she could let go. She no longer had to bear the cross of her mother and sister. The amount of grief that Deborah was living with over the loss of her loved ones had taken over her life.

The movie ends with knowing that Mrs. Henrietta's family were never compensated for the use of her cells. And Deborah passed away.

After watching the movie twice, I sat back in devastation. Did Deborah die of a broken heart? Was the life that her sister lived in the mental institution that straw that broke her emotional camel's back? Was the information she received about her mother enough for her to finally let go and rest? Or did those unresolved feelings cause her to pass with unresolved feelings for the people who harmed her loved ones?

It is my belief that we as people often take on burdens that we should give to God. We become hoarders of pain and suffering. Holding on to experiences and circumstances that we can't change or control.

In my early twenties and up to the present day, I started laying my burdens at the Father's feet in prayer. Meditating on His word (scriptures) instead of focusing on things I couldn't change.

One of my favorite scriptures to pray when a situation is grieving me is Matthew 11:28-30, "My yoke is easy, and My burden is light". In this passage Jesus was speaking to people while traveling to different cities, spreading His message.

Jesus told the people that they didn't have to bear their own burdens, that He was sent by God the Father to carry the weight of life for them. All the people had to do was believe in Him and give their worries to Him.

This scripture has comforted me so many times in my life when life started life'n and I would worry about my circumstances. Have you ever had this experience? Has God sent you a message telling you that "He got you?". Well, if you haven't had that experience yet, let this chapter be your first time. God's grace blankets your heart and soul when you are sad, depressed and even stricken with grief.

God reminds us that His grace is sufficient (2 Corinthians 12:9). So, I ask, why are you still holding on to the past and pain, when you possess the option to let it go? God's grace ushers in an atmosphere of healing that will comfort you in your time of grief.

Prayer/Declaration

Lord, I declare that You are the beginning and end to everything in my life. Take this situation/circumstance from me. I release me from the burdens of my past, and the things I cannot change in my present. I allow You to do with these things as You see fit. I'm letting go and accepting Your grace while I ask for your mercy. I thank You for what You've already done in my life.

I also look forward to seeing what You have instore for my future. I give You my pain that Your grace will transform this grievance into thanks and praise. I declare that I will see victory from my grief, in Your mighty name I pray, Amen!

Exercise

I challenge you to write down everything that might still be haunting you. Place the scriptures from this chapter beneath those grievances. Then go to your bible or google scriptures on grief that speak to your circumstance/or situation. Get it all out. Once you've written it all down, speak the previous declaration over yourself.

You should praise God right now! You have begun your Journey to Freedom. Hallelujah! 👣

Grace & Gratitude

Write It Outside-of-You!

For by *grace*
You have been
saved through faith,
And that not of
yourselves,
it is the gift of God.

Ephesian 2:8, NKJV
Grace

Chapter 5
Graceful Expectations

I met and married my ex-husband in my early thirties. By this time in my personal evolution, I knew who I was as a single woman. I was aware of who I was in my walk with Christ. I knew who I was as a friend and family member, coworker, teammate, and any other role that I was currently maintaining. What I knew then and will cosign on now is, I was ready to be a WIFE.

I deliberately posted pictures and scriptures on my vision board of Ephesians, chapter 5. For those who don't know, this chapter speaks of walking in love, light, and marriage. I was praying for me and my homegirls to be blessed with our Boo's; or as we say now, B.A.E. (Before Anyone Else). I was deliberate about my thoughts and emotions towards joining my life with my potential mate.

I'd stopped entertaining my ex's, or dudes I knew didn't qualify to be my "next" blessing. Not to leave out, I was also super busy in my professional life.

I was gearing up to face and complete my final year of graduate school. Single, saved and living a servant-girls' life. I was that good God-fearing, encouraging homegirl who verbally talked people through their issues. And yet, I was unfulfilled. I wasn't meeting my own personal expectations for my own vision of my life.

How was I able to encourage everyone else, and yet I was down in my spirit regarding my expectations of my love/family life?

Now, anyone who really knows me knows that I love people. I also love **Love**. I get joy from seeing people find each other and unite as a couple. I'm also surrounded by successful married couples in my personal life. So, it's only fitting that I would want such an experience for myself.

During this waiting period, I found myself getting low in spirit. I wanted to know if marriage was written in my life's book chapters or not. My career and school were already check marked on my list of accomplishments, but I was still feeling unaccomplished.

Grace & Gratitude

Then I heard God asked. "What about My plans for you? Did you forget? Has your patience run out for My ultimate plan?".

I felt bad. Even guilty. Because if I was being honest. I grew impatient with God's plan. I was getting weary in my well-doing, lol. I felt so ready for my next level of New. New beginnings, new possibilities, new Love! My heart and mind were wide open, (like the 91 freeway during quarantine); for new possibilities. I was Open, Open, Open… like the old Mervyn's commercial for new jobs and new love. Emphasis on the Love 😉

I had my life as a wife all figured out. I would marry a man who loved me and desired me as his wife. He would be the perfect accessory to my already established dream life. We would go to church, pray together, pray for each other, and accept each other; flaws and all.

There would never be any fights unless it was simply for the purpose of making-up later (wink wink). 😉 We would be blessed and live happily ever after!

I had crafted all this carnal perfection up in my heart and mind that I wanted for myself. Then I realized; I'd left God out of the equation. I just knew for sure that God was gonna bless me with the perfect man for me.

My man and I would have no real problems. The sex would be spectacular, and I was committed to doing things God's way in this next relationship. At least that's what I'd told God in my prayer time for the 50-leventh time, lol…

I just knew that whoever was my next man, would be the One. We would walk hand-in-hand into the warm and toasty California sunshine, telling everyone around us that, "God did it for us. God brought us together. God made the path clear and straight for the two of us to find one another". In the end, we would come together to build this great life together.

Now don't get me wrong, you should always be prepared to receive the greatness and blessings that God has for your life. However, don't be so laser focused on what you desire out of your life that you don't leave space for God to do what He does 😊.

It's cool to expect and prepare for God to bless you, but if you are so adamant at narrating your story and building unrealistic expectations of what your life will be, you will be unable to see and receive God's glory for your life. I'm not gonna preach to you right now. I'm just going to tell you about how grateful I am that I offered my expectancy up to God.

That last year of graduate school that I mentioned earlier, I was stressed out about finding a job after graduation. I was obsessed with making sure I was networking with the right people that could further my career in social work. Not to mention that the year before, I had spent the entire school year rehabbing from a horrific lupus flare.

My heart and mind were literally all over the place. But all I could think about was, "Lord I just want a family. I want to be a wife and a mommy. I want my husband and children to call me blessed. And if I must give up my career to receive my legacy… Lord, do your thang".

When anyone would ask me what I wanted to do after I completed my master's program, I'd lie and give them the response I thought they want to hear.

> "I want to land a good job and help other professionals earn a better working wage in the field of social work".

Now to be fair, I did then and even more now, desire that dream and goal for my fellow social workers and behavioral health professionals. However, my hearts' desire was to get married and grow a family. I didn't want people to rain on my parade, so I offered up my politically correct answer.

What God revealed to me is this:

Personal Expectations (or the opinion of others) suffocate God's plan and purpose for your life. You must stop going with the flow of what you think everyone or even what you've planned for your life. Often, the plans you've drawn up for yourself don't even measure up to God's glory that awaits you.

So, take a pause while charting your own course and go to God in prayer. Allow His purpose and promise to become the blueprint that you choose to follow.

When I think about my life up until now, I've made many of my life's decisions based on the approval of others. I've done what people told me I should do, instead of asking God to order my steps. Then one day, I became sick and tired of being sick-and-tired, and I went to God in prayer and meditation. I asked God to open my eyes to His plan for me.

In the bible days whenever someone started walking in the expectancy of God's will for their life, God gave them a new name.

So, I went to God during this transformative period and asked Him to change my name. I wanted to be made new. I wanted to see myself and my life the way He saw my life playing out. I wanted to wait on Him with expectations of greatness.

Grace & Gratitude

From that day forward my thought process totally changed. Even though I valued what my friends and family thought about my decision-making process. God's directive outweighs everything that is presented to me.

Take note of this scripture because I will mention it a few times in this book. God has had to repeat it to me on replay so many times in my evolution.

Jeremiah 29:11-14, I will paraphrase this passage but feel free to read the scripture in its entirety-

> "11) For I know the thoughts that I think towards you, says the Lord, thoughts of peace and not of evil, to give you a future and a hope. 12) Then you will call upon Me and go and pray to Me, and I will listen to you. 13) And you will seek Me and find Me when you search for Me with all your heart. 14) I will be found by you, says the Lord…"

Pray- So now I prayed this prayer:

"Father God, help me to make the right decisions for this season in my life. Let my yes be Your yes for me. Allow my no or not right now, to aligned with Your will for my life. Lord.

I don't want to do anything that you do not approve of. I don't want to accept a position, take a trip; or even entertain a friend, acquaintance, or potential mate that is not God-Approved. Thank You in advance for my transformation. In Your mighty name I pray, Amen!"

That prayer request changed my life by changing my heart of expectancy. I no longer desired jobs, friendships or love interests that didn't' align with God's will for my life.

All the dead-end relationships that I was entertaining fell away from me. I no longer carried them around like the "bag lady" that Erykah Badu sings about.

Grace & Gratitude

As I allowed God to clear out the bad connections and stinking'-thinking in my psychological and emotional makeup. I felt my heart expanding for new opportunities.

I discovered that God was showing me His expectations for me. He was developing my ability to be still and trust His perfect will for my life. All I had to do was say yes to doing things His way by trusting His plan instead of going so hard with mine' and the expectations of those around me.

Now let me tell you the grace-of-it-all. I had worried myself into a tizzy for nothing. Had I just held on a little while longer I would soon meet my first husband, land a job right out of graduate school, and start the next phase of my life covered in God's unmerited favor.

God's grace made my life easy-peasy. I just had to trust His timing and align with His will instead of my own. And that's what I want you to do. Let's go to God in prayer, then we'll get to the exercise portion of this chapter and write this thang out 😉.

Prayer

Heavenly Father, I come to You understanding that You already have a masterplan for my life. I don't take for granted that You design a path for me based on how You love me and care for me. I thank You for covering me with Your grace. I am also grateful for the opportunity to live out the promise you have for my life.

Lord, give me the patience and courage to walk the path that You have created for me. When I become impatient or discouraged, grant me the strength to wait on You. I love and honor You. In Your mighty name I pray, Amen!

Exercise

Now take some time to jot down some instances where your expectations either line up with God's will for your life, or where you need help waiting on the Lord. Don't be afraid to dig deep. Not all desires are right in your face.

Don't worry about anyone else's thoughts and opinions of what you should desire for your life. Whatever comes to mind, write it down and submit it to God in prayer. I can't wait to see what He does for you.

What to Expect... Expect the Best!!!

2 My brethren, count it all joy when you fall into various trials,
3 knowing that the testing of your faith produces patience.
4 But let patience have it's perfect work., that you may be perfect and complete, lacking nothing.

James 1:2-4
Gratitude

Chapter 6
Immeasurable Grace

By now you've come to the realization that I'm talking to you like we're sitting face to face. This is also how I converse with God. No lie, lol…

Growing up as a child of two young parents who divorced before I was born. I thought every child grew up with just one parent in the house. Matter of fact, I was shocked to get older and see so many kids around me came from two-parent households, lol… Crazy right!?!

My mother is such a phenomenon to me. I have watched her provide for the five of us. Sometimes working upwards of three jobs, while delegating tasks and responsibilities to her village to help with us with our kids, if need be. And she did it all with so much grace.

God gave her the strength at 22 or 23 years old to humble herself and receive help from those who were willing to help her in raising her kids. With all the different hats she wore, I started to question what was so unbearable about my bio-dad that she decided she'd rather live a life as a single mother than remain married to him.

I looked at my mommy as Super Woman, as a child. If I'm being transparent, she still is today. Present day, I've gone through my first marriage, with only one child and life is hard! Lol! I can't even wrap my mind around raising and feeding five little personalities and their bottomless bellies.

My mom had minimal to no help with bills and other responsibilities. And when it came to receiving child support, there was no such thing as direct deposit; so, if my mom wanted to receive the child support check from my dad, she had to go pick the check up from him.

Unfortunately, my dad didn't make the transaction easy. There was always negative or discouraging words from my dad; however, my mom didn't return the same energy.

My mom remained calm, picked up the check and often times drove away with tears in her eyes, or a look of anger and frustration on her face.

With all that being her experience, she never spoke ill of my dad to us. Whenever it was time for us to visit for a holiday, she took us to visit with his side of the family until we could drive ourselves. No matter how she was greeted or ignored, she took us.

Me now having been married, I realize how graceful my mom was when interacting with my dad and his side of the family. As for me personally, I'm not as close to the cross as my mom, lol… I still haven't developed the same level of grace that God has so generously gifted my mother.

I let people know, "I'm 3 feet from the cross and if someone pushes me too far. They might get these hands or a few "Sunday-school-words" that my Granny Green would blurt out whenever us kids would push her too far, lol… It would take the Holy Spirit flooding me with His presence for me not to act a fool 😊, Ting!

But Grace!!!

Grace & Gratitude

God showed me His grace by how my mom handled her interactions and response to my dad. What I learned by my mom's actions is…….

You must own up to your own **Actions**, **Words** and **Responses** to everything in your life. My mother never once told us kids about how badly my dad treated or spoke to her. If she did react to his negativity, I never saw it.

Other than the somber look on her face when she left his presence. Her meekness speaks to my spirit to this day. Being that I'm still working daily to lay down the gantsa in me, I'm not sure I would have been so calm as my mom was when I was little. Especially not my 20-year-old self.

It's as if grace was her cloak and shield. The amount of energy it took for her to do the back-and-forth routine and conversations with my dad never took away the positive energy she used to continuously love on the five of us kids.

Grace & Gratitude

My mom served at the church and maintained her friendships with her homegirls; while still being a loving daughter, sister, and mother. All while pushing through the negative interactions with my dad.

God was super good to my mom by providing a way out of that toxic relationship. She didn't feed the negative force that was trying to entangle her. And yes, I said "Entangle" 😁

You see if you let Him fight for you. God will fight your battles while keeping you in perfect peace. God provided the resources and support that my mom needed to keep herself and her children going.

Let me remind you that she was 22 years old while divorcing my dad. And as I said before, I do not currently embody the same level of grace that my mom has shown my dad, lol… So please, Try Jesus and not me ☺.

My mom never returned the bad words and disrespectful energy that came from my dad, she simply surrounded herself with people that could protect and respect her peace.

In return, that's what she offered my dad when she had to physically interact with him. My mother most definitely exemplified immeasurable grace with this relationship. If my mommy could do it back then, I know for sure I can do it now. So, my question to you is this. What's going on in your life that you need immeasurable grace to deal with?

Prayer

Let us pray. Dear Heavenly Father, I come to You humbly asking for the strength and direction I need to graciously walk and live through the situations I've been struggling with. Please help me to apply a Luke 22:42 spirit over my current circumstances. Help me to show love even when I'm receiving hate and negativity. I thank You and I praise You. In Your name I pray, Amen!

Exercise

Let's make a list of those things that you need immeasurable grace for. Write down the people or circumstances you're facing that will require the abundant grace of God. After you complete your list, just sit back, and watch God do His thang.

What does Your Grace-Metric Look Like? 😉

11 For the **grace** of God that brings salvation has appeared to all men.
12 teaching us that denying ungodliness and worldly lust, we should live soberly, righteously, and godly in the present age.
13 looking for the blessed hope and the glorious appearing of our great God and Savior Jesus Christ.

Titus 2:11-13
Grace

Chapter 7
God's Grace Produces:
The Fruits of the Holy Spirit

"Lord, Thank You....... You sacrificed your life to redeem me of my sins. I'm grateful that You carried out Your assignment without questioning the Father's plan. You healed the haters and ate with prosecutors. You did all these things even when you knew people would betray You. Help me to develop a heart like yours. A heart full of the **Fruits of the Holy Spirit**. That my words and actions only flow in **Love** and **Kindness**.

That my **Longsuffering** and **Gentleness** carry conversations that my physical person dares not try. That **Forgiveness** and **Temperance (Self Control)** be ingrained in my DNA. That Jehovah Shalom (God of Peace) goes before me in every conversation and interaction, so I don't offend and only deposit **Peace**. I choose to exude **Goodness** and grace from this day forward. Amen."

I felt like I had to start this chapter off with a prayer, reciting some of the fruits of the spirit because life can really work on your nerves, lol!!! Sometimes you can even feel like God doesn't care about you. However, when you dedicate time to learning, understanding, and practicing the fruits of the spirit; I know that God can renew your heart and mind to live this thang out in peace.

In the beginning of the book of Galatians, chapter 5; verse 16 – the passage starts off with the difference between walking in your flesh (or man's/woman's nature) or submitting to the fruits of the spirit. Let's see what the scripture says.

> 16 So I say, live by the Spirit, and you will not gratify the desires of the sinful nature.
> 17 For the sinful nature desires what is contrary to the Spirit, and the Spirit what is contrary to the sinful nature. They are in conflict with each other, so that you do not do what you want.
> 18 But if you are led by the Spirit, you are not under the law.
> 19 The acts of the sinful nature are obvious: sexual immorality, impurity, and debauchery.

20 idolatry and witchcraft; hatred, discord, jealousy, fits of rage, selfish ambition, dissensions, factions.
21 and envy; drunkenness, orgies, and the like. I warn you, as I did before, that those who live like this will not inherit the kingdom of God (Galatians 5:16-21, NIV).

When I was a babe in Christ, I always heard elders in the church talk about the fruits of the spirit. How we as youth and young adults were supposed to practice living by these scriptures. I found myself rolling my eyes and my neck saying, "I'm gonna do unto others as they do unto me". Oh, how immature and naive I was.

As I grew older, I realized that I had no desire to treat people the way they'd treated me. It took too much time and energy to do so. Why lie because they lied. What would I gain from cheating on a boyfriend/fiancé/ or husband because they cheated on me? What would be the point on returning a harsh or disrespectful word to a coworker or stranger who hurt my feelings?

Maybe you can tell me what I could gain from matching someone's "ugly energy" towards me with being "uglier".

If you don't know me well, let me say this about myself. I don't believe in being ugly for anybody. It took me too long to become cute, lol!... I digress...

I started digging deeper into the **Fruits of the Spirit**, that reads as-

Galatians 5:22-25, NKJV:

> 22 But the fruit of the Spirit is love, joy, peace, patience, kindness, goodness, faithfulness.
> 23 gentleness and, against such things there is no law.
> 24 Those who belong to Christ Jesus have crucified the sinful nature with its passions and desires.
> 25 Since we live by the Spirit, let us keep in step with the Spirit.

Now this section of the chapter really spoke to me! I might not speak with such eloquence, but I carry this thang in my heart y'all!

I'm choosing to walk and live these characteristics every day. And when people encounter me, I pray that they feel at least one fruit of the Holy Spirit residing in our interaction.

At the end of the day, I want to be right in God's sight. I want my spirit to read Love, Joy, Peace, Gentleness, Kindness, Longsuffering, Faithfulness, Goodness, and Patience. Whether I'm with my family, friends, church members, coworkers, future employees, or even strangers. I pray my aura reads God's grace.

My Story

When I worked as a residential counselor fresh off receiving my bachelor's degree in psychology, I remember working with a few managers and supervisors who weren't that nice to me. If I'm being really real, they were mean. To this day, I don't know what the beef (problem) was that they had with me.

However, I knew there was definitely a problem by my work schedule. You see, there were two women in charge of making the work schedules for all staff that worked in all the agencies' three locations.

I had been working at the agency for about six months or so; and the residents and staff seemed to really like me. I guess the manager and supervisor didn't like that. Now, I didn't realize it then, but my presence served as a threat to them.

The residents liked me. I got along great with all the staff at the agency. Not to mention that I also had the education and degree for upward mobility. Maybe they saw me one day taking their jobs?... I'm not sure. I was just doing my job and enjoying working to the best of my abilities.

Then one day my dream job turned into a nightmare. The scheduling manager and supervisor called me into the office to discuss a schedule change.

It was told to me that staffing was changing and therefore my schedule would change as well.

I would now be working all Sundays and alternating between morning and evening shifts throughout the week. Now the manager and supervisor knew that I was an avid church attender and that by changing my schedule I would no longer be able to attend church.

I would also have to forfeit singing in the choir. Which was something I shared with the residents at the agency. Since my schedule was all over the place my activities outside of work would cease to exist. I was angry, discouraged, and shocked that this was happening to me.

	1st & 3rd	2nd & 4th
Sunday	3pm-11pm	7am-3pm
Monday	7am-3pm	
Tuesday	-	-
Wednesday	3pm-11pm	
Thursday	-	-
Friday	3pm-11pm	
Saturday	7am-3pm	3pm-11pm

At first glance, this schedule doesn't seem too bad, right? But here's the kicker. I lived an hour away from the agency, so the women knew that the constant switching of shift time-blocks would wear me out physically.

The new schedule swallowed up an additional 2 hours in commute time every day. I was exhausted. I live with this schedule for several months until one day I asked the supervisor if we could revisit changing my schedule to something more consistent. Preferably all 7am-3pm, or all 3pm-11pm. I explained that due to the schedule alternating between morning and night shifts, I wasn't getting the proper rest I needed to take care of myself.

A sinister grin appeared on the supervisor's face as she then asked me, "Is this position beginning to prove to be too much for you, Charnyce? Do you think that you should work somewhere else? Maybe you should consider working closer to home." After that meeting with the supervisor, I realized that not only did she not like me, but she was also trying to get me to quit working for the agency all together.

I remember telling my mom and my friend Ricco what was said in the meeting. My mom said, "weigh your options Charnyce. Start looking for you another job closer to home."

Then Ricco's response was, "Snooty, f#xk that woman. You have a degree, look for something else; then bounce! Matter fact, do I need to come up there!?!" I quickly answered, "No Ricco, I just need to vent to you right now, lol."

Ricco is my best male friend. And my go-to "profanity-guru". This man will place a combination of words together that will have you begging for mercy, lol…

I remember feeling so broken in my spirit. I was finally making headway with my newly acquired degreed profession. I could see myself growing in this agency, and now this roadblock was blocking my forward motion. I couldn't continue with the schedule that I had because it was physically running my body low.

I was still growing in my relationship with Christ, and I didn't understand that this was really an act of spiritual warfare. However, what I knew for certain was that I could go to God with anything that was weighing me down.

So, I went to God in prayer. I asked God to order my steps and show me what to do. I knew that He'd seen me struggling with this schedule and I was growing weary.

Amid all my uncertainty, God sent me a third conversation that would serve as confirmation. I was complaining to my coworker Marvin, that I couldn't keep working this crazy wishy-washy schedule. That the schedule was physically and emotionally wearing me out.

Marvin said something to me that made me realize that our conversation was God-ordained. Marvin said, "Sister, don't complain about this schedule thing anymore, you are well educated. Start applying to new jobs somewhere else." And then my inner light bulb lit up like a Christmas tree during the holiday season.

Grace & Gratitude

God sent me a confirmed word by way of my Mom, Ricco, and now Marvin. It was time to stop focusing on that crazy schedule and be the best employee I could be while looking for a new job elsewhere. So that's what I did. But during that 6 month stretch God granted me peace.

The agency ended up hiring more staff, which allowed me to receive a full morning schedule. That 7am-3pm schedule also meant that I had to work with that manager and supervisor closely for a long stretch of time. However, during that process I began exercising Love, peace, kindness, gentleness, self-control; and every other fruit of the spirit while working so close with both women.

It was amazing to say the least. I stopped feeling so tired. Matter of fact, I had supernatural energy with the joy to match.

Then one day my coworker Marvin told me that our friend Susan had taken a new job at another agency, and I should see if they were hiring. I reached out to Susan and indeed the other organization was hiring.

I forwarded my resume to Susan immediately. I interviewed for the position 7 days after submitting my resume. I received word that I got the job 1 week interviewing for the position. God's timing felt like lightning speed-

After receiving good news from the new agency, I could breathe easier. I knew that it was time to move to my next opportunity. I had learned what I needed to learn educational and work wise at the first job. And I had also grown spiritually.

God's grace covered and carried me through that scheduling nightmare. And I was able to be kind when the enemy was trying use that manager and supervisor to run me low.

During that trying time in my life, I meditated on the Fruits of the Spirit. God used that interaction with that manager and supervisor to deepen my understanding and utilization of His Fruits. With that dedication to becoming my best self, I was able to sit at the table with those women or work in the same environment and exude Love, Joy, Peace, Patience, Kindness, Goodness, Faithfulness, Gentleness, and Self-Control.

In my last month at the agency, I decided not to wild-out (I would have been well within my rights if I did though, lol). I went to work every day that last month handing out compliments and good mornings and afternoons to those women who were trying to stunt my growth.

I learned through that experience that you can't embody the fruits of the spirit without them being tested and tried in your life.

I was in the midst of some serious hater-ation, that I'm sure no one would have faulted me for going off on those women and quitting that job. But that's exactly what the enemy wants you to do. He wants you to forfeit your blessings by giving up and quitting on yourself.

I'm here to tell you, don't give the enemy satisfaction. Instead of cursing that manager and supervisor out and quitting that job. I listen to wise counsel, went to God in prayer and walked in the fruits of the spirit while I waited for my next blessing to materialize. I encourage you to do the same.

Don't throw in the towel. Employ the fruits of the spirit. Allow God to work through your hardships.

Now, I know that applying this practice to your life may prove to be a tad bit difficult, but I know you can do it. Look at all the things that God has brought you through so far. You can do this!

Prayer

Heavenly Father, open the eyes of my heart. Help me to search myself to identify which fruits of the spirit best suit me in this season of growth. Lead guide and direct me as Your word challenges my very nature. Help me to say no to myself as I say yes to You. In your name I pray, Amen.

Exercise

Now I ask you. Do you desire to display the Fruits of the Spirit? If so, which one speaks to you at this moment. Write down each fruit that catches your eye and why it stands out to you. Now go forth employing those very fruits in your life. I already know your testimony is gonna be amazing!

Grace & Gratitude

What's Your Fruit Cookin' Like?...

"Do not sorrow,
For the joy of the
LORD
Is your strength."

Nehemiah 8:10
Gratitude

Chapter 8
Overwhelmed to Overjoyed!

"When my heart is overwhelmed, lead me to the rock that is higher than I." (Psalm 61:1-4). This scripture played over and over like a song on repeat flowing through my wireless speakers.

A year or so after getting married I was experiencing pain in my stomach. Or should I say my womb. Making love to my husband was a chore. I didn't understand why my "Hello Kitty" (nickname for my vagina) wasn't happy.

God had finally blessed me with a husband. It was supposed to be on and crackin' in the love-making department. It was time to pop my booty on a handstand. But nope. Too much pain, too much discomfort.

I was scared to tell my hubby what was going on with me physically. Our sexcapades became fewer and fewer throughout the week. When I just couldn't endure the pain, I would say things like.

> " I'm exhausted babe. Can I give you a cookie I.O.U.?"

Or something like,

> " I can't tonight, it's a lupus thing".

Anyone who's known me long enough know that I never pull the lupus card. Especially if I don't have to. So, hubby didn't press the issue. I still felt horrible about the whole thing.

Days turned into weeks, and he no longer approached me about getting intimate at all. I couldn't tell if he was tired of being turned down, or what it was. I just knew I had to be proactive. I then made an appointment with my OBGYN and explained the symptoms I was having.

> "Hey doc, something is going wrong down south. My Hello Kitty is on hiatus. And I'm trying to keep my husband."

If you're wondering if that's how I talk to my doctor's, the answer is Yes. I'm a straight shooter. My doctor examined me and delivered some discouraging news.

"Charnyce, your last pap smear came back with possible stage 2 cancerous cells. Those cells are most likely causing your discomfort or pain. I would like to do a colposcopy today to check if there is a possibility that you have cervical cancer. I know you said you haven't been sexually active in a few weeks. That's good. You will need to hold off on sex for an additional 3 weeks after this procedure today".

The doctor had me undress from the waist down and she performed the colposcopy. Each scrape of her scalpel was worse than the first. Although the doctor numbed the area that she was collecting the tissue samples from, this procedure hurt like heck!

When the doctor was done collecting her final swab she said, "You will most likely fill some heavy cramping today.

So, you may want to take some Tylenol once the local anesthetic wears off. I will check back with you in a few weeks with the results. Until then, get some rest and remember; try to abstain from coatis until after the results are in."

Dang Gina! I said to myself in my Martin Lawrence voice. This doctor is killin' my vibe! Do she know how many rings I turned down before saying yes to my husband. She is trippin' with this don't have sex at all thing'! (#Rollin'MyEyes). However, I surely wouldn't being having sex for the rest of that week. I felt horrible in my southern region.

A few weeks had passed, and I returned to the gynecologist exhausted and overwhelmed to say the least. My body didn't feel right, and I knew something was up.

I had received a letter in the mail from my doctor's office stating that the test results still displayed the same results at the pap smear. The doctor stated that she wanted to perform a more intrusive procedure called a LEEP and she handed me some research on the procedure.

Now I was scared.

What was really going on down there. I asked the gynecologist if this was normal to perform a second colposcopy or this LEEP procedure? She insisted that we do the procedure again to check to see if the cancerous cells were still showing as present, or the LEEP in hopes of catching this issue before it turned into a problem.

Just when I thought that things couldn't get any worse, lupus woke up and decided to pay me a visit. When lupus decided to rear it's no-edges-havin'-self I was fit to be tied. Why was this happening to me? I did not need this type of drama in my life right now. I had just gotten married! Why Lord, why?!!

Six months had passed, only to return to the doctor's office for more bad news. The lupus flare exacerbated the symptoms I was having with my "Hello Kitty", and we would need to take more drastic measures with treating this issue. So, the doctor offered two suggestions for treatment. I could undergo an L.E.E.P procedure, or I could get a hysterectomy. LEEP stands for loop electrosurgical excision procedure.

The treatment is used to eliminate cancerous and abnormal cells found within the cervix or vagina. The LEEP procedure would lessen the chances of me being able to have children in the future. However, the hysterectomy would ensure I'd never be able to carry my own child naturally.

You know, with the total removal of my uterus and all. Either procedure or surgery seemed like death to my legacy, and therefore I didn't want to do either one. But I had to choose something, or I was afraid, I'd never be able to physically enjoy being with my husband again.

The doctor kept trying to sell me on the fact that I could always adopt children or remain a "good auntie" to my nieces and nephews and not worry about birthing my own children.

Then, just to kick me while I was down, she threw in the remark: "You are getting closer to geriatric pregnancy age. And we don't want you to be at risk for preeclampsia or still birth."

Grace & Gratitude

I was starting to dislike my gynecologist. Just when I thought she could bring me no more bad news, she struck the final nail in the coffin of our patient-doctor relationship.

The doctor then suggested, "Let's put you on birth control, because I'm just too afraid that you will get pregnant and end up passing during labor; or your baby wouldn't make it to term."

Now I know I had spoken to my gynecologist before about not using birth control, due to me being a stroke survivor in the past. My team of doctors had recommended that I never take birth control again for that reason alone. And for those of you who don't know, the use of any type of birth-control in pill form, shot or implant can place women at risk for having a stroke.

The visits with this doctor and her unsolicited advice were chipping away at what little patience I had for her and her professional opinion. I was tired of hearing bad news after bad news. And even worse treatment recommendation after recommendation.

Lord, Please help me, please? ...

I left that doctor's visit boggled with grief. I felt the pressure of the doctor's suggestive treatment plans on one shoulder, and the weight of not being physically available for my husband: on the other. I agreed to go through the LEEP procedure. It seemed to be the lesser of the two evils.

The week that I was set to go in for the LEEP procedure, I felt like my future was at stake. Like the treatment would not only not cancel out the cancerous cells that was showing up in my pap smear; but I would soon loose my new husband and my future ability to have kids in the future.

As I laid on the exam table waiting for the doctor to begin the procedure, I prayed,

> "God, please be with me. Block any danger that tries to come to harm me. I praise You right now for the victory. I know that no weapon formed against me shall prosper. Have Your way during this procedure today. I lay this situation at Your feet. Please give me peace while in this valley. In Your mighty name I pray, Amen".

I guess the doctor noticed that I was praying because she waited until I opened my eyes to begin. Then she asked, "Charnyce are you ready?" I gave her a thumbs up as I placed a set of goggles over my eyes. Then the doctor pulled her protective shield in front of her face and began the procedure. I didn't feel any pain because the doctor had numbed me with a local anesthetic. When the procedure was done, I was relieved to be going home. All I could think about was…

Will I be able to enjoy sexy time with the hubby after this ordeal was done? I also questioned if I'd be able to have children later down the line? So many questions danced the two-step in my mind. I was in total wonder. The procedure was successful and after a few more weeks I would be able to get back into the swing of things with my hubby.

Two months have passed, and hubby and I were back to black love. I was feeling good and more confident than ever. God had answered one of my prayers. I was still married and back to showing my man how much I loved him behind closed doors. But what about the future.

Would I be able to be a mommy someday, or had the procedures stolen my legacy from me? I had done all the research for surrogacy and storing eggs for future endeavors, but those options were beyond my reach.

To be honest, they were out of my tax bracket. In addition to the cost of someone else carrying my child for me, my team of doctors worried that retrieving eggs from my body would cause more harm than good. Seeing that I had fibroids, and I was closer to forty than I was to thirty. Urgh!!! I was still so unimpressed with my circumstance! Then that feeling of being overwhelmed hit me again.

> "Lord, please help me to focus on giving thanks in this time of uncertainty. I thank You for restoring my ability to be physically loving with my man. Help me to look to the hills for which cometh my help. When it comes to my ability to be a mommy. I know that my help comes from You, and Your path for me is greater than my circumstances that are in front of me. Quiet my heart Lord, so that I can hear You, Holy Spirit.
>
> Guide my feet as well as my thoughts. In your mighty name I pray, Amen."

My prayer that day carried me into a new mindset for the next stage of my life. As I began to lean more on the Fathers' shoulders and rest in His grace for this trial in my life, He began to fill my life with joy. I was able to stop focusing on the doctor's reports and suggestions.

I asked Jehovah Shalom to give me peace and help me to stay calm and settle in God's restorative joy. I knew then as I practice now that happiness is a fleeting feeling. But the joy of the Lord makes me strong (Nehemiah 8:10, NKJV).

As far as if I was able to have children… Take a moment to go on my social media platforms. You'll see how God's grace has blessed me. 😊

Prayer

Dear Heavenly Father, I come to You seeking a peace that out ways my ability to understand. I ask that You search my heart. Help me to look to You when life is coming at me from all directions. Allow me to see me through Your lens. I want to walk in Your grace and be thankful for each step of my journey. In Your matchless name I pray, Amen.

Exercise

Now it's your turn. What are you facing right now that's making life impossible for you to walk in the joy of the Lord? What words can you muster up to give that thing over to God, while giving Him thanks and praise? Write that/those thing(s) down. I'm so proud of you.

What is "Pressure" vs. "Joy" for you?

Here I am, God,
arms wide open….
Pouring out my life,
Gracefully Broken ….
My heart stands
 in awe of Your name
Your mighty love stands
strong to the end
You will fulfill Your
purpose in me
You won't forsake me;
You will be with me.

                        Tasha Cobbs-Leonard
                              Grace Project

Chapter 9
The Elevation of Gratitude
~Thankfulness~

" Great is Your mercy towards me. Always providing for me. Great is Your mercy I see. Great is Your grace…" (Psalm 86:13- {chapter title}- "Prayer for Mercy, with Meditation on the Excellencies of the Lord", NKJV).

The lyrics of this song by Donnie McClurkin took up space in my heart when I hit my late 20's to early 30's. Up until a few years ago, I had the feeling that I was **arriving to life's party, late** 😖 . It was as if I was receiving my blessings so far behind the curve of others around me. I couldn't see my life's progress for what it was. The thoughts in the back of my mind were …

> "Lupus is going to kill me before I get to do _____.

Or,

> "I'm gonna meet Sweet Baby Jesus before I accomplish "this" or "that".

I was so anxious to move like other people around me were moving in life, that I couldn't see the forest through the trees of my own life. I spent so much time focusing on what I hadn't accomplished due to living with lupus and being a voyeur in other lives', that I didn't stop to think about how far God had brought me. Also, what He'd brought me through.

Then something happened. One day while I was busy hitting the Holy Spirit's line like a love-sick teenager, I could hear God say;

> *"Come unto Me, and I will give you Rest..."*, (Matthew 11:28-30).

I felt some type of way at first. I was definitely in my feelings. I felt a little guilty, like I was annoying God. Or maybe I wasn't trusting Him enough?

I thought that I was doing all that was required of me. I was fresh off taking leave of an entire graduate school year while rehabbing from a lupus flare. I literally spent a calendar year on hiatus from living life (working, churching, and hanging out, school, work, Everything....), to recover from the flare up. When I say I was jacked all the way up; I was tore up from the floor up.

During the flare, my liver and kidneys were failing. However, God was right there. Miraculously, around the three or four-month mark of rehabilitation; I began to hear the Lord say,

"*I am renewing your strength*" (Psalm 27:14; 2 Peter 3:9).

God The Father was literally healing me from the inside of my being, while restoring my outer appearance. Each trip to the laboratory or the doctor's office, my test results read miraculous improvement.

With that being said, the doctors would agree to decrease my medications or take a medication off the regimen list. My team of specialists couldn't even understand how I was able to rebound in the way God was showing up in my body.

The brain fog and sleepless nights that I was experiencing due to high dosages of certain medications started to clear up. I slowly returned to my weekly workouts. I was also strong in spirit and clear-minded enough to run my own errands and take back physical control of my everyday life.

Within two months of that encounter, I was strong enough to get out of the house and start moving-and-shaking in the community with no one driving me or retrieving a wheelchair to transport me from one place to another.

I was now able to physically attend church. My time spent singing the songs and worshiping through church services began to restore my body, even the more. I started really feeling myself by this point.

Due to my restored physical and mental strength by God, I was able to return to serving in the church. Singing with the praise team and choir, as well as mentoring with the youth and young adults. I felt my "Help" coming on, as the elder saints use to say 😊.

When it came time to return to my graduate school program, I ended my service with the youth ministry so that I could focus on finishing my last year of graduate school. I was really sad about that decision, but God was doing something **new** in me.

God carried me through 6 master level classes and two part time jobs; that would assist me in paying the overage of the program fees to complete the requirement of my graduate school program on time. I was booked-and-busy. What more did I have to give?...

Then I heard the Holy Spirit say,

"What about your Gratitude..."

It took me by surprise. Had I not been showing how much I appreciated my Lord and Savior? Was I walking around with an ungrateful heart? Oh, my goodness. How embarrassing!...

How could I ask God for something and then give myself all the credit when the ball start rolling in my situation? How could I forget to honor Him with a Thank You.

I started beating myself up emotionally in my devotional time. Apologizing to God for my ungrateful heart posture. I remember praying to Him and asking for healing and getting my life back on track. But I couldn't recall telling God, Thank You.

I didn't get to wallow in my pity party too long before the Heavenly Father reminded me that He was right beside me in my valley of insecurity. Then He told me.

"I have not given you the Spirit of fear, but of love and a sound mind." (2 Timothy 1:7).

Wherever you are I am there also (Psalm 139)."

One day after arriving to campus, I turned down the music in my car and sat in silence. I allowed myself to be in the moment and allow God to speak to me. I had created this list of life events that I wanted to achieve that had been ruminating in my thoughts. During that meditation time I started releasing my time frame from that list. My conversation with God went a little something like this:

> "Father God, first and foremost I want to say Thank You. Each day You've breathed the breath of life in me and given me strength. You've blessed me to begin yet again with this diagnosis of lupus. You've granted me the time and space to heal emotionally while restoring my body. You've renewed my mind and focus.
>
> You've also allowed me the space to gather my thoughts and wits to return to school. I'm sorry for taking the credit for Your healing process, Father God. Please forgive me for not telling the doctors and anyone who asked that You (God) healed me.

Thank You for Your grace and mercy. Thank You for Your peace, Jehovah Shalom. From this day forward I give You the praise and publicly credit You for the blessings and restoration poppin' in my life. Thank You so much. Amen."

Let me tell you! That prayer in the car that day catapulted me into the stratospheres of my walk with Christ and life. When I acknowledged God with that **Thank You**, my little timeframe and the pressure that accompanied it, disappeared.

God allowed me to focus on completing my graduate school program, while blessing me to look and feel good throughout the process.

Instead of me looking on social media wondering when my life events would become "post-worthy". I instead was living a life of thanks and praise. This mindset blessed me to thrive in a busy season of my life. I hope my experience inspires you as well. 😊.

My commute time to school and work became my praise and worship devotion time with God. My health was poppin'! My spirit was buss'n! My sense of gratitude was focused on the One who had carried me into this great space in my life.

What was my take-away from this lesson of *Gratitude*? You must be patient and praise God through the process. Your faith must also be tested (1 Peter 1:7). You must believe that God has the best intensions for you, (Jeremiah 29:11).

That He's working life out for your good, (Romans 8:28). When you start to thank God and stand on His word, you will experience God's goodness in your life. You just have to acknowledge Him with a heart of *Gratitude*.

Prayer

Dear Heavenly Father, thank You for Your patience. Thank You for writing a script for my life. Thank You for blessing me with Your promises at the right time and season of my life. Lord, please don't take your grace and patience from me. I desire to receive what You have for me. I want to walk in Your will for my life.

Help me to develop a heart of gratitude. Remembering that life is more than post-worthy reels. Remind me of the many blessings that You have already provided for me. I desire to always have a thank You on my lips for You. In Your mighty name I pray, Amen.

Exercise

Okay, now is the time for you to write down some desires that you have yet to see manifest. I want you to give them to God. Write down a Thank for each item listed. Remember that a Thank You God can change the trajectory of your life.

Thank Him Before It Happens 😉

"The Lord bless you
and keep you;
The Lord make His
face shine upon you,
and be gracious to you;
The Lord lift up His
countenance upon you,
and give you peace."

Numbers 6: 24
Gratitude

Chapter 10
God's Pace of Grace

I'm a big fan of journaling and vision board development. I think that's where God began to strengthen my writing style and organizational approach to telling my story. I have spent the last 20 + years writing down everything from my: thoughts, feelings, dreams, desires, medical wins, losses; and even my diet and sleep patterns. The food intake and medication regiment were strictly for tracking my progress with lupus flare recovery. However, I noticed a pattern that I had to ask God to help me break.

> "Lord why am I scribing my every move? It's so tedious? Annoying too? At least the medical stuff. Help me understand what I'm doing and the reason to keep doing this?

As my writing style developed into my late 20's through my early 30's; I heard the Spirit of the Lord say,

*"**Write the Vision Charnyce** (Habakkuk 2:2-3). **Your gifts will make room for you** (Proverbs 18:16).

Then the Holy Spirit whispered, "**I have not forgotten about you**". I thought for sure God had placed me at the back of His mind while He was busy blessing everyone else around me. I'd watched friends, family and even strangers on social media: set, post about and achieve goals that I too wanted to reach. Feelings of doubt settled in my heart and mind. Then I had the feeling that God had truly forgotten about me.

God then had to remind me of His process of developing me. Countless medical procedures and hospital scares occurred: heart attack, stroke, and organ failure. Deliverance from heartbreak that I thought would literally take me out! Advancement opportunities and job loss that I'd taken for granted while trying to do His job on my own. And all of this before the age of 30.

Those events weren't even on my radar. However, that's what God had brought me through. I had to stop counting other peoples' blessings and focus on HIS promises to me.

Many days and nights I would cry. Initially tears of doubt or defeat. Frustrated and wondering what was taking God so long? I know I was doing what God wanted me to be doing? Minus a few fallen moments. For the most part, I was an angel, "Ting! 😊." And still God never threw my indiscretions in my face.

The Holy Spirit would one day affirm my tears, though. I would then realize that I needed to activate my faith with His initial request. I wrote the vision He gave me down on paper. The dreams that were revealed while I slept. The visions that came to me while I rehabbed from my sickbed. I also had to speak out loud the dreams He showed me and the hope that I had in my heart.

> "I believe every word you told me, God. I believe You will bless me again. You will heal me, again. I will love, again. I will laugh in my heart, again!"

That's when I created my first detailed vision board. Yes, this board looks like any board you've ever created at one of those manifest your destiny events. It's amazing! However, I put a little Jesus-Sauce on my board. I placed related scriptures next to the desires I had in my heart. After I placed God's word alongside my hearts' desires; I prayed to God the Father asking that He only materialize those personal desires that aligned with His will for my life.

Now you would think that I would say that God blessed me with everything I placed on my vision board right away, because I honored Him by placing His scripture on my board. But that's not the reality. Well at least not right away, *Ting* 😊!

The real Tea is this, after you make your request known to the Heavenly Father (Philippians 4:5-7), you must wait on the Lord to respond (Romans 12:12; Psalm 27:14). Waiting for revelation can be a hard task, no matter your relationship with Christ.

I found myself falling into seasons of doubt and worry while waiting. It was like the devil and my fallen nature crept in at times, and it was annoying too.

For me the doubt was like an ole, tired boyfriend saying things like;

> "Hey girl, what you been up to?
> "You still waiting on God to answer your prayers?"
> "Why don't you let me be your Calgon and take you away for a quick minute?"

Then right before I was about to take a bite of the forbidden fruit and entertain that ole' tired dude… I would hear God voice affirming me saying, (Isaiah 55:8-12)

> 8 "For my thoughts are not your thoughts, neither are your ways My ways," declares the Lord.
>
> 9 "As the heavens are higher than the earth,
>   so are My ways higher than your ways and my thoughts than your thoughts.
>
> 10 As the rain and the snow come down from heaven, and do not return to it without watering the earth and making it bud and flourish, so that it yields seed for the Sower and bread for the,

11 so is my word that goes out from my mouth: It will not return to Me empty but will accomplish what I desire and achieve the purpose for which I sent it.

12 You will go out in joy and be led forth in peace; the mountains and hills will burst into song before you, and all the trees of the field will clap their hands.

Now I ain't no preacher, but I knew it was God confirming His word for my life. So, I kept charting my dreams. Praying and asking for guidance from the Holy Spirit. I deleted those numbers out my phone of those dudes that would be major pitfalls. I didn't attend events that wasn't edifying to my relationship with God. I became laser-focused on following God's instructions.

And what do you know, my access was granted through that act of patience and obedience. The Lord Jesus provided the understanding of the scriptures that I had been placing on the vision board. The anxiety that I once felt when witnessing others live out their dreams became an encouragement for me.

I began to settle into my own life and realize that God's timeframe for me was different. That didn't mean that my blessings were not coming. It meant that I would be 100 percent ready when my blessings started to flow.

All I had to do was **trust, believe, be patient**; and **activate my faith**.

I had to commit that passage of scripture to my memory and recite it every time that ole hater Satan tried to play me out. The devil was trying to shake my faith, but God was with me.

Often times we get caught up with what we see. We watch people post their news reels on social media and television. We cheer so hard for them, that we forget to keep track of our own blessing.

What we must remember is God's timing is not our timing. He knows when to bless us with that job. That house. That relationship. That car. That baby. That next opportunity.

But sometimes it requires us to wait on Him. Trust what He's shown us and block out anything that doesn't look, or sound like HIM.

You see God is limitless. Just when you're ready to give up, Stand. Stand on His promises. When you begin to stand on His word for your life, you will catch the rhythm for His pace for you.

Prayer

Dear Heavenly Father, thank You for the opportunity to hear from You. Holy Spirit, please continue to let peace flow over my spirit as the Father is developing His purpose and plan for my life. Give me the passages that speak to my particular journey. That I may meditate on them and allow each scripture to become a part of me. Thank you, Lord, for your guidance. In Your Name I pray, Amen.

Exercise

What are some of the life events that you are waiting on God for? Write them down. Then go to your bible or on google. Search for the scriptures that speak directly to your life and desires. Once you have written it down or placed it on your vision board, give it to God. Watch out, God might just blow your mind 😇.

God's Pace vs. Yours?

You are fairer
than the sons of men,
Grace is poured
upon your lips.
Therefore,
God has blessed
you forever.

Psalm 45:2
Grace

Chapter 11

Gracefully Broken

I'm one of those people who loves "Love". I like seeing those posts on social media that say, "We're not perfect, but we're perfect for each other."

For some reason I just love reading that phrase. But what happens when you find yourself on the downside of that phrase? I'm a strong-willed individual, however; when relationships in my life look like they are headed for the grave, my heart breaks. I become this sad little girl inside who beats herself up emotionally for letting the connection go down the drain.

Over the years I've tried to circumvent the breakup process. Telling myself that I wouldn't connect to anyone I thought could potentially end in separation. But that was that "little girl" being unrealistic.

Grace & Gratitude

The Holy Spirit revealed to me that all relationships are not final. That the connections that end, was meant to be.

"Sometimes God has to break your heart to save your life." Shout-out to Pastor Jameliah Gooden, (Unity Church International; North Carolina). That's her line that she says on a regular 😉.

The first time I heard Tasha Cobbs', "Gracefully Broken", my heart fluttered. I was immediately filled with peace. I didn't finish listening to the song before falling to my knees, to bow in prayer. I started thanking God for all the mistakes I'd made in my life that He molded into messages that I now share with you.

The truth is, I've been **through** a lot of interpersonal relationship pain. Some of the pain was self-imposed. Other experiences were God's way of strengthening me in different areas in my spiritual and emotional development. What I know for sure is that, if God brought me to it; He would give me the grace to live through it.

Now, I'm not going to lie to you; many times, my feelings were hurt when dealing with the different heart aches and disappointments I've faced. I've also had a bruised ego, a time or two. But I wasn't destroyed when things turned out bad. God was with me every step of the way.

I remember this time I was dating this guy in my late 20's. I don't know what really attracted me to him because he wasn't my normal "type". He had a swag about him that was cool. But it didn't move me. He had money, property, and a couple of nice cars.

Those were all things I was used to when it came to my romantic interests. But then there was his voice. You might be thinking, "Charnyce you fell for the dudes' voice." Yeah, I did. But it wasn't his speaking voice that caught me.

The dude could sing. Let me rephrase that.
This guy could, sang. He would hit a note and my heart would flutter. He would sing a vocal run, and next thing I knew I didn't have any panties on.

Excuse my truth….

If I haven't said it before, let me make the statement now. I'm not one of those super-saints. I'm 3 feet from the cross. And yes, I've had the "We fall down, but we get up "moments in my walk with Christ. That's what also qualifies me to speak on God's grace the way that I do, *Ting! * 😊 .

Coming from a family that can sing. It was fun conversing with the guy about songs and favorite genres of music. Every phone conversation or physical date was something to look forward to. We would text each other lyrics from songs that made us think of one another. It was some old school black love simulated moments going on.

Oh, you caught that, right? Yes, I do mean simulated. You see, there was no love in this relationship. It wasn't written in the Holy stars. It was all lust and trickery. The truth of the matter is that I entertained this guy in one of my "bored" seasons of life.

God had intentionally set me apart from the dating scene for a large period of time, so that He could teach me some things about myself in the spirit realm. However, I couldn't see the blessing of being "set apart"; so, I went and started entertaining the serpent and eating the forbidden fruit.

I was Eve, but this guy wasn't Adam. This dude was more like the serpent; so-to-speak. The dude's words started out cunning and sweet. He never missed an opportunity to distract me with that singing voice either.

There would be times that I would spend the night with him, (Yes, I know I was all the way wrong. Just follow me for a moment). I would wake up to do my morning devotional time with God. I would hear the Holy Spirit telling me that I was wandering away from God.

The next thing I knew, ole boy would interrupt my "devotional time" with a 90's song, pulling me back to the bed. And guess what, I wouldn't stop him! I would pause my prayer session in get right back in the bed.

Then on my way home or to school. I would spend the entire time asking God for forgiveness, while blasting my gospel music all the way to my destination. I was entangled with this dude for almost a year. The majority of the time doing this drive-of-shame of my way to wherever I was supposed to be for the day.

Then one day the fun stopped, and the drama began. Singer-Boo and I had a disagreement. He'd tried to do what he always did and interrupt my morning devotional time. However, this time I didn't oblige him. I had intentionally gone in the living room with my bible and began to pray.

He found me in child's pose position, kneeling in prayer with my bible in front of me. He'd asked me what I was doing, as if he couldn't see me bowed in prayer.

Annoyed, I ignored him and tried to remain in my prayer position. He tried rubbing my shoulder to get me to break my position. Still, I didn't budge. Then the unspeakable happened, he grabbed me and said,

"Didn't you hear me talking to you?"

I felt my gansta rising in my spirit. My right eyebrow arched like Dwayne "The Rock" Johnson, and I turned to look him in the eyes.

> "I'm praying right now. Give me some time and I will be with you shortly"

I said to him in my calm voice. I returned to my child's pose position, but my spirit was now in defense mode. I could feel him walk away as I acted like I was still praying. My peaceful morning with God had turned into a love song gone wrong. My devotional time with God was ruined, and ole boy was trippin'. I didn't know if I should go into the room and try to get some clarity with him; or gather my things and just go home.

I did what I thought the Jesus in me would have me to do. I went into the room with a calm tone and asked what was going on. Singer-Boo had started gathering my things, stuffing them into my overnight bag.

When I noticed that he was upset I tried to touch him. He swatted my hand away and rudely handed me my travel bag. I could hear him muttering something about me choosing my God over time with him.

So, I slid on my shoes and headed out the front door. On my way home I didn't play my gospel music like I normally do. I began to pray aloud.

> "Dear Lord, I know You saw what just happened. I was minding my own business, trying to carve away some alone-time with You. Then this dude barges in and gets all swoll-in-the-chest about me spending time with You. Now I know he's not my man and I'm not even supposed to be engaging in the physical with him. But I thought we at least had an understanding about my relationship with You.
>
> It's like he was upset and jealous that I was spending time with You. Lord, please show me what path to take in this connection? In Your name I pray, Amen."

Now, I'm sure God was shaking His head while listening to me pray about this situationship. I had willingly engaged in a relationship with Singer-Boo. I had knowingly taken time away from convening with God to sing sweet nothings with ole dude. I'd even broken my vow of chastity while in relationship with this guy.

Now he has an attitude when I want to spend time with God. I did in fact catch what he said. He had the audacity to say **My God**. Like, now all of a sudden, he doesn't believe in God!!! What was I doing? Why was I neglecting my relationship with God to appease this dude? I had been trippin'. I didn't even love this guy. I was just passing time.

That's when the Holy Spirit said to me,

> *"In your boredom, you turned away from Me and entertained a foreign spirit. You allowed a soul tie to be formed and neglected quality time with Me. Do you see that this relationship is not for you? Come back to Me. Remember My love. This is not what you should be doing right now. Your love-story will not be this."*

I felt bad for myself, for a quick minute. I know I knew better than to fall into the lust trap. I couldn't believe Singer-Boo was trippin'. I had spent the past year sex'n, sing'n and going out with this dude. And this is how the connection ends? I mean, I couldn't keep hanging out with him now. I'd had this conversation with the Holy Spirit, and it was confirmed that Singer-Boo was not my Boaz. So, I needed to cut him off and move on.

Besides the fact, I had fallen off course with God. The crazy part is this interaction with Singer-Boo wasn't the first tell-tell sign that I was entangled.

There were a few red flags that popped up during our time together. However, I'd chosen to ignore them for the time being. But nothing comes between me and Jesus Christ.

So, after a few heated conversations and hurt feelings later, the situationship was laid to rest. I'm saying it calmly now, but it ended pretty bad (you'll have to wait for the book on my personal journey for the details on that story 😊). Let's stay on task for God's grace for now.

As I was saying, the situationship ended with me and Singer-Dude ceasing all communication. It wasn't so much as a text, call or dove in the air. We just stop contacting one another. Usually, I would feel bad when I stopped talking to a guy. But him saying, "Your God"; rubbed me the wrong way. Beside the fact that I had broken my vow of no-sex.

How dare he be so disrespectful. He knew I loved God. He knew that my relationship with Jesus Christ was real. He'd come to church with me and everything. How dare he say such a thing!

I had to stop myself from making Singer-Dude the villain because real life was, I was at fault too. I laid my morals and discipline down by the riverside the day I decided the lay in bed with Singer-Boo.

Or maybe the compromise was the times I went out with him instead of spending some alone time with God. I allowed my fallen nature to take control of the steering wheel of my life, and now a year had passed, and I had nothing to show for it.

Then one day, while on my way to school I heard a song. Tasha Cobb's gracefully broken was playing. I immediately tapped repeat on my pandora app. When Tasha spoke about God breaking you to place you on the right path. It hit me.

When the situationship with Singer-Dude took a turn for the worst, he'd started speaking insults and disrespect, instead of sweet nothings. That wasn't love. That was Singer-Dude's real feelings and thoughts about me. I had created a soul tie with a man who didn't care about me. That was a problem. Now I had to ask God to help me solve it.

I'm not one of those people who tends to leave things unresolved. If I don't mess with you no more. I want you to hear the **breaking news** from me. I don't want you to assume that's why I ceased all communication with you.

Needless to say, I grabbed my phone to contact Singer-Dude because I wanted him to hear the words come out my mouth.

But God blocked it -

As the phone rang, my snappy attitude softened. I felt the Holy Spirit wash over me and I ended the call. I didn't need to state the obvious. The connection was left-on-red, and that was all that needed to be understood. There was no need to exchange words with ole' dude.

As gracefully broken played on repeat in my mind throughout that time, I focused my attention back on God. I found myself repeating apologies at nauseum. I wanted God to know how sorry I was for entertaining strange fruit and going against what I knew was right.

The peace of Jehovah Shalom now rested on my heart, and I was grateful that God was so gracious even when I was disobedient. The Holy Spirit reminded me that He is always with me. Even when I'm off my path (Psalm 139:7-10). I was simply happy to be back in good standing with the Heavenly Father.

I could no longer practice the "live to love again" so loosely. I no longer desired to leave myself open to self-inflicted hurt, loss, and disappointments. I now decide to be intentional about each relationship that I entered into.

On the flip side, there's great rewards and the possibility of being amazed beyond your wildest dreams. Being a "Hopeful Romantic", whenever one relationship ends, I'm usually gearing up to connect with the next person.

Whether it's romantic love, friendship, or business endeavor, I'm here for it. However, it's a bit tough to rebound from; especially if you experience disappointments, back-to-back.

Every time a relationship meets its end, I'm usually all jacked up. However, the way my God is set up. I now know that God has my back. Even when I fall all the way off the proverbial wagon. Instead of beating myself up for making the wrong choice; or engaging in the wrong type of relationships. I go to God with a broken spirit and contrite heart (Psalm 51:17).

Prayer

Let's pray. Dear heavenly Father. I have to admit I'm nervous, but I am open to trust You with my heart. Forgive me for my wrongdoing. Help me to get back on the path You've laid out for me. I understand that Your correction and redirection is designed to make me strong. Thank You for turning my mess into a message that I will one day be brave enough to share with others.

I honor Your graceful approach to directing my path. Help me to forgive myself when I get off course and return to developing a closer relationship with You. Help me to be okay with the things and relationships that don't go my way. In Your name I pray. Amen!

Exercise

I want you to write down a person or relationship that you've been in where things didn't go how you imagined it would. How do you process your feelings towards that experience in a healthy way? Have you written your feelings down? Maybe you've shared these things with a friend or confidant? Have you taken it to God?

In Micah 7:19; the passage says, " God cast your faults into the sea of forgetfulness." Then in Isaiah 43:25, " the Lord says, He crosses out your bad deeds for His own sake. Never to be spoken about again. If God will do these things for you, then you need to forgive yourself and get back up and try again.

Love again...
Trust again ...
Try God again!...

He said if you try Him, he will open up a window and pour you out a blessing that you won't have room enough to receive (Malachi 3:10).

Now usually this particular scripture is used by fundraisers, however; I'd like to challenge your heart in this chapter. If you are ready to experience God's wonderous works in your life; allow His grace to help you live a life of love and grace.

Grace & Gratitude

Write Your Grace Journey...

You are enriched
in everything
for all liberality,
Which causes
thanksgiving
Through us to God.

Corinthians 9:11
Gratitude

Chapter 12
A Prayer of Serenity

Oftentimes we take on tasks that we should be giving to God. We find ourselves biting off more than we can chew. Overcommitting ourselves in different tasks, relationships, jobs etc. Today I want you to ask yourself a few questions.

- Why did I not say I need help?
- Why didn't I accept the help that was offered?
- Am I afraid to succeed?
- Am I embarrassed to fail?
- What is holding me back?

One prayer that stands out to me is the Serenity Prayer. Let's read it together.

"God, grant me the Serenity to accept the things I cannot change.
The courage to change the things I can; and the wisdom to know the difference."

This prayer is most synonymous for being recited at addiction recovery meetings. However, the poetic prayer derived from a man name Reinhold Neibuhr, who authored the original text. I wish Mr. Niebuhr was still with us. I would love to know what inspired him to write such an inspirational ploy to God. This prayer is so sincere and beautifully poetic.

Whenever I find myself in a pickle, I recite this prayer. I most often speak this prayer when feeling overwhelmed.

One time I was in a lupus flare, and I had really committed to doing every single thing the doctors ask me to do. They advised I take salt totally out of my diet to decrease the amount of inflammation I had in my body. So, I obliged them.

I wrote down everything that occurred each day. I even wrote down my meals, trips to the bathroom, hours of sleep and my weight each day. My health became my full-time job. However, I was unable to do anything outside of logging my progress for treatment.

The doctors' appointments, lab draws, strict dietary regimen, and sleep schedule left me with no time to do anything else. Days, weeks, and months went by. In the end, no progress. In fact, my lab results showed that the lupus flare was getting worse and beginning to attack my liver, as well as my heart and kidneys.

The doctors wanted to increase the medication and introduce even more medications that would affect my ability to have children. Lupus was, once again taking over my life, and my usual cry to God didn't seem to be working. I was praying,

> "Lord, Jehovah Rapha; please heal me from the top of my head to the sole of my feet."

I felt guilty for reciting this prayer so much. I didn't want God to think that I didn't believe in His power to heal me. Then one day, me and my Siamese-Twin, Latoya went to the Christian bookstore by her house.

While looking through the shelves I stumbled upon this candle with the Serenity Prayer recited on the front. The candle had a clean smell, and that prayer seemed to be calling me.

I didn't really have enough money to buy the candle and the bible that I went in the store to purchase. So, as we finished looking around, I took my bible to the counter to pay. Toya came behind me and said,

> "You forgot your candle."

I replied,

> "It's okay Toy, I'll get it next time. My money is a little funny, and my change is strange, lol."

We smiled at each other, and I proceeded to pay for my bible and waited for Toya by the register. Toya placed her items on the counter, and then she placed the candle on the counter as well. Then she said,
> "Just think of this as a late birthday present. I can see that this really means something to you. The bonus is, I also have a coupon!" 😊

We both laughed. The cashier rang up her purchase, and the two of us grabbed our bags and walked to the car.

When I arrived home, I went straight to my room to pray. However, this time I prayed a different prayer. I took the candle out of the bag, lit the candle, and recited the **Serenity Prayer**.

> "God grant me the serenity to accept the things I cannot change,
>
> The courage to change the things I can,
> And the wisdom to know the difference."

As I recited the prayer repeatedly, I could feel the power of the Lord washing over me. All the weight and stress from my daily medical regimen started to lift off me.

I didn't feel the heaviness of my daily routine bogging me down, like in days past. I wasn't worried about the people who questioned the dedication I had to my health; nor the doctors who seemed to be doubting what I said about my lifestyle changes.

I stopped thinking about the people who said I wasn't praying the right prayers, or that I didn't believe that God was a healer. Yes, all these things really happened.

What the serenity prayer showed me; was God was giving me grace and mercy. I had to give my cares and concerns to the Lord (1 Peter 5:7). No matter whether it takes a day or a lifetime to catch this message, God will change your life. You see, His grace is what cemented that serenity prayer on my heart.

I asked God to take the burden of the lupus flare off me. It was starting to overwhelm me, and in turn the flare was getting worse. But if I could accept the fact that I had done what I could to address the flare. Then let go of the parts that I couldn't control, then that was all I needed to do. God had my back.

Days, weeks, and months went by. Then one day, I received lab results through email that the lupus activity was decreasing. Then my kidney doctor followed up with a voicemail stating that I no longer needed to take certain medication because my lab results showed no lupus activity.

I mean, I could've told the doctors that that's what was happening because my life was "hitting" different. I was able to drive myself to appointments and run errands, On My Own!

I had enough energy to get back to my workout routine and cook my own food. I was taking showers by myself. And without a shower chair. I even had enough spunk to beat this cute little face of mines with no breaks. I was really starting to look like, ME! That's how I knew for sure, that God was restoring me. I felt great and I was still standing.

Prayer

Father God, grant me the serenity to accept the things I cannot change, the courage to change the things I can; and the wisdom to know the difference. In Your mighty name I pray, Amen.

Exercise

Now it's your turn. Write down an event or thought pattern that you've had that you've needed God to help you through. Whether the matter is present day or in the past, lets hand it over to the Lord and recite the Serenity prayer over that thang.

Your Personalized "Serenity Prayer"

Grace be with
all those
who love our
Lord Jesus Christ
in serenity.
Amen.

Ephesians 6:24
Grace

Chapter 13
Grace to Know You're "ENOUGH"

After graduating from Cal State San Bernardino in 2003 with a bachelor's degree in psychology; I thought that conducting therapy and counseling sessions would be my contribution to society. I dove headfirst into the social services industry, which truly broadened the lens of how I saw my life's service.

While working in the field; I operated in many different functions. I served as a family paraprofessional, residential counselor, case manager, therapist, employee trainer and policy writer. In each position, I encountered many people, male and female; that possessed some struggle with self-worth and self-awareness.

See, I love people, and my personal optimism and self-assurance has always been a viewpoint that I've chosen to share with others. My work life would be no different in my approach.

My initial thought process was that if people could see what I saw in them, their little lightbulbs would turn on! They would be: Better, Stronger, more Confident; Empowered! That was very green and cute of me.

The reality is…. while engaging in treatment, you often start to peel back layers of people's pass and uncover brokenness, insecurity, false sense of self, maladaptive behaviors; and so on and so forth. There was also the presence of generational curses adopted and applied after years and years of being told; you are not enough.

No matter what population, gender, religion, or sexual orientation of the people I was working with. Client after client. Session after session. Visit after visit. There were always variations of the same conversation.

I would hear how the client had been indoctrinated with falsehoods fed to them over and over again from different family members, doubters, and debaters who told them that they weren't **Enough**.

My inner child and young-adult-self connected with them all, each and every time their sentiments mirrored my experiences and past emotions.

My Story-

Growing up with not much interaction, and no conversations that I could recall with my bio-dad. The therapy sessions regarding parent-child relationships hit close to home.

I knew I was a good person, but for some reason, that wasn't enough. My prayer life became inundated with the hearts of my clients and the questions and cries of my younger self.

I would be crying out to God in my quiet time asking what I could say to assist and comfort my clients. He first sent me to Psalm 139.

I knew that God the father knew me before He formed me in my mom's womb, but I needed Him to reassure me in my encouragement of others, and my younger self.

God simply told me that He would be with me in my high and low places in life. And that I could find rest in Him. That He would guide me in my treatment plans for my clients. And that everything that He placed inside of me was ENOUGH. That I'd gone through the experiences with my bio-dad and lost relationships to simply offer comfort for others who would otherwise give up. Or even worse, threaten or try to take their own life.

God was always right there reminding me… HE consistently fed me the words to give to His people. The ones that believed and even those who were non-believers… His grace was sufficient and everlasting. The Holy Spirit would whisper sayings like:

"I will not leave you as orphans, I will come to you." John 7:39 ESV

"I know the plans I have for you, to give you a hope and a future" Jeremiah 29:11 NKJV

"But the helper, the Holy Spirit, whom the father will send in my name, he will teach you all things and bring to your remembrance all that I have said to you. (John 14:26, ESV).

Prayer

Dear Heavenly Father, I come to You needing a little reassurance. I understand that You said in Your word that You are here with me, but I'm having a hard time releasing all the negative talk and experiences that I've endured throughout the years. Help me, Father God. Help me let the old go. Help me to believe and walk in the mindset of being, Enough. In Your mighty name I pray, Amen.

Exercise

Have you ever wondered if you were enough? Or maybe you had an experience that made you feel less than. Well, let's write it down. Because it's time to give it to God. Now let's release ourselves and walk this thang out in Jesus name!

Grace & Gratitude

My "Enough Phrases"...

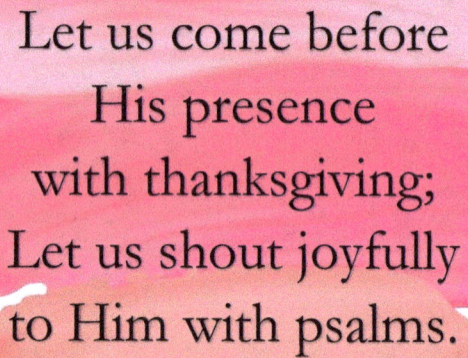

Let us come before
His presence
with thanksgiving;
Let us shout joyfully
to Him with psalms.

Psalm 95:2
Gratitude

Chapter 14

Faith to Move Mountains

My mom's dad (Granddaddy Wilford) is from Florida and he's number 3/or 4 of 13 kids. There were two sets of children born to his parents and of course him being number 3, he falls in the first set of children born to the flock.

Well in the second set of children, there's a sister named Hazel. Auntie Hazel was small in stature much like the siblings said their mother was. However, her personality was as tall as Shaquille O'Neal, lol. She was a real powerhouse. How I met and experienced Aunt Hazel will be an encounter I'll never forget.

My great aunt Nell, one of my grandmother's sisters, had passed away, so the Cali family flew to Florida to pay our respects. While we were in town, we were introduced to my grandfather's younger siblings. That's when I first met Auntie Hazel.

She was chocolate skinned and petite. Most importantly, she was a force to be reckoned with. The family had put together an impromptu service for the Cali family, and it was an encounter I'd never forget.

During testimony service Auntie Hazel shared her testimony of deliverance. She did not look like what she'd been through; that's for sure. She spoke about how God would deliver you from your own hands and still do so in **Grace.** After we'd all prayed and were getting acquainted with each other, she asked me did I have something to share.

I told her about me living with lupus and how long I'd had it. Auntie Hazel looked at me with an intensity that you had to be there to believe. She then asked me if I wanted to be healed. I had a puzzled look on my face because my guess was that everyone wanted to be healed. She then said to me, "You have to believe and decree that you are healed!"

Then she just kept repeating while placing her hand on my chest. "You got to Believe it. You got to Believe it".

Auntie asked, "Baby, do you believe God can heal you?" I paused to think and said, Yes. Auntie Hazel then said,

"HE will not fail you". She hugged me, greeted my sister standing next to me and walked away.

Her words have been settling in my spirit ever since. It was the grace of God that carried Auntie through her past of addiction and dependency, to recovery. She and her husband were able to rebound from their past and adopt two children from the foster care system, that had no place to call home.

Aunt Hazel and her husband Lonnie started a church and was aiding others who'd lived with addiction and dependency issues. Helping others to take back their lives through Jesus Christ.

I only met and spoke to Auntie Hazel that one time, but I know for sure that that one encounter was all I needed. God orchestrated that brief conversation that would shift my viewpoint of faith and its connection to God's grace.

If God could take the taste of addiction out of Aunt Hazel's mouth, then He could heal me from lupus or anything else that I was struggling with. All I had to do was believe in His ability that was within me. Even if God never took lupus away, I had to start living like it was already done. I would also have to start thanking HIM in advance.

Truth be told, HE inhabits the praises of His people (Psalm 22:3). And when you believe and thank Him, He shows up. So, I went to my bible and looked up scriptures that spoke of faith and deliverance. But instead of writing down those scriptures, the Holy Spirit gave me this Acronym for "**FAITH.**"

F. follow God's lead

A. acknowledge His presence in all you do!
I. inhabit- Live with a heart a praise for his grace.

T. thanksgiving- honor Him with appreciation

H. Hallelujah- Praise Him even when you can't see your way through.

Exercise

Now, you might develop different words for your FAITH acronym, and that's perfect. Because I want you to deepen your relationship with the Heavenly Father. Take some time out today and try your hand at filling in the FAITH letter blanks. What do you come up with?

Prayer

Dear Heavenly Father, I come to you with mountains standing before me that I don't have the strength to move. But I believe that You can do anything for me. I will accomplish whatever you've placed in my heart for me to do. Come into my heart oh God. Accept my praise and thanks. Help to conquer the current mountains in my life. In Your mighty name I pray, Amen.

My Mountain-Moving Grace looks like...

Grace & Gratitude

He inhabits the
praises
of His people.

Psalm 22:3
Grace

Chapter 15
Finding Gratitude

Some people might assume that finding gratitude would be an easy task. You think to yourself. your prayer life is poppin', so you think that you're covered on the daily talks with God. But what if I told you that you're just doing the bare minimum. Each and every day, you have to choose happiness.

You have to practice being grateful or thanking God for everything good and bad thing in your life. Charnyce, what you mean "good and bad? I ain't about to accept no negativity in my personal space." I can understand why that would be your initial reaction but check this out. If you never experienced negativity, how could you truly identify positivity in your life?

Gratitude starts with accepting that even when your day isn't going the way you thought it should, you still can muster up a "Thank You Lord."

Grace & Gratitude

I like to start my day off with prayer, meditation, journaling, affirmation; or something of the sort. I even listen to some of my favorite music, or one of my favorite pastors speak while I work out.

You see, gratitude doesn't look the same for everyone. Offering God, a gift of thanks doesn't have to be over the top, but it must be intentional. You have to greet God with an open heart and mind every moment you get a chance.

As a lupus survivor of 20+ years, I make a conscious decision to tell God "Yes), each day. Seeing that I'm naturally optimistic, you would think that I would have the Jill Scott, "Living my life like it's golden"; song on replay each morning in my head.

However, it's sad to say that that's not the case for me. On the days when I wake up on the wrong side of the bed. Or if I receive bad news, I have to give myself the pep talk. I make a declaration like,

- " This is the day that the Lord has made. I will rejoice and be glad in it!" (Psalm 118:24).

- If I'm feeling low in spirit, I say. "I am the head and not the tail. I am above and not beneath " (Deuteronomy 28:13)

- When lupus tries to rock my block, I say. "Lord, you make all things work together for my good." (Romans 8:28)

You may not believe this is what I do, but it's true. I slap God's word on every nook and cranny of my life. No matter the situation or circumstance. I encourage you to do the same.

It don't matter where you are when you give God thanks, either. If you're dropping the kids off to school, thank God while in the drop-off line. If you're sitting in traffic on your way to work. Thank Him while you're staring in the back of all those taillights in stop-and-go traffic. If you work from home and your computer is taking a while to turn on, say a quick prayer of gratitude while the computer gets itself together.

I remember being a baby-saint and thinking I had to come to God all super formal for Him to acknowledge my praise and thanks (Hebrews 13:15). Then I realized that God made me, and He knows my heart, as well as my intensions.

So, even when I wake up on the struggle-bus and I can't find the words to say. If I offer up a "Thank You Lord for waking me up this morning." That's enough for God.

I won't lie and say that it's easy for me to have a praise on my lips. Often times, when I'm presented with a problem; like I said in a previous chapter, I too struggle to find the silver lining in my situation. But God is my "go-to." When I don't know how to react to a situation, I look to Jesus; and He helps me (Psalm 121:2).

I thank God in advance for what He's going to do. As well as what He's already done.

I once heard a pastor say, we often use God, like aspirin. We feel ourselves getting a headache from one situation or another and we begin calling on God to save the day.

Much like finding the pill bottle and popping two pills in our mouths and chasing them with water.

We start hitting God's line when we need something. But what if you could go to Him with a thank you when you don't have a problem? What if you started greeting God with a Hey Lord how You doing for no reason at all?

I think the Lord would feel like us women feel when we receive flowers for no reason. He would be surprised and pleased. Excited to interact with you. Waiting to gift you with an unexpected blessing. He would be on-the-ready to give to you. Even when you don't ask for anything.

Sometimes, when I'm going throughout my day, I just stop and say Thank You God. But I had to grow to a level of emotional maturity to be able to thank God without asking for or receiving something in return.

Take a few minutes by yourself and start finding moments where you can speak Gratefulness over your life.

For me, gratitude created a peace over me that transformed the lens that I see my life through. And we all know how difficult it can be to achieve and maintain peace.

It's as if you have to be deliberate about your practice of gratitude. You might even find yourself resighting the cliche phrase like, " Making lemons into lemonade."

Or, if you're not a believer in Jesus Christ; maybe you call on whomever your higher power is to help you. It takes a person with an open heart to humble yourself enough to know when to call on the Lord. Even when it's something as small as praying that your day goes well. That's how you begin to find a sense of gratitude.

Finding Gratitude (='s) Claiming Your YES….

I remember back in 2018, I had been hearing a lot of the word "No". I heard it so much that I had made up in my mind that I was reclaiming my favorite word, "Yes". So, when the lupus flare that I was coming out of seemed like it wanted to rear it's ugly head. I started to recite,

"Father God, I thank you that I'm healed from the top of my head to the sole of my feet".

My finances were low, I declared, " **The Lord makes me rich and add no sorrow"(Proverbs 10:22)**.

Me and my husband wasn't seeing eye-to-eye, I'd say, **"Lord I claim peace and joy over my house"** (Ephesians 4:2-3).

And the last thing I would say is. **"This is the year of my YES!"**

After these declarations, I started praising God for what He had already done in my life. I then rejoiced in advance for the YES that was ruminating in my spirit. Next thing I knew, as my heart and mind opened up; so, did the doors of my life.

One random Friday afternoon while I was working my cosmetology apprenticeship job, I received a voicemail from my kidney specialist stating that my blood work showed no lupus activity was present. Which meant I was in remission. It also meant that I would no longer be taking the medications that treated an active lupus flare.

A few months after that, I passed the state board exam for cosmetology and became a licensed cosmetologist. The very next month, I found out I was pregnant with my son, Chance!

Now I could shout right NOW!!! Do you see how claiming your Yes and practicing gratitude can turn your life around!?! This thang really works. But you gotta put your hope and thanksgiving on that thang!

No more thinking about what happened in the past.

No more focusing on what's going wrong in the present.

Just start telling God Thank You. Even if your whole life is givin', Blah!!!

I am a living witness, that if you begin to praise and thank God before the good starts poppin' off in your life. It will come to past! Amen Amen Amen! I feel a Hallelujah in my spirit on this chapter. I'm praising God for you right now!

Prayer

Let's pray over this thang! Dear Heavenly Father, I am petitioning You on behalf of me activating my YES season. Help me to stand on Your word. To apply a heart posture of praise and thanks over my life. Help me to look to You and thank you for simply being in my life. I want to develop a stronger heart of thanks, whether You bless me or not. I want to arrive at a "Any way You bless me, I'll be satisfied" spirit. Thank You in advance for helping me develop a heart of thanksgiving. In Your name I pray, Amen.

Exercise

What steps are you willing to take to activate your Yes? Write them down right here. Also take some time out to write down what you are grateful for. Remember, once you've found the gift of gratitude, it's up to you to walk in it.

Grace & Gratitude

Hey Gratitude...
I See You 😊

Great is Your mercy towards me, You have delivered My soul ….

Psalm 86:13
Gratitude

Chapter 16
Guard Your Heart:
(Grace + Mood = God-Vibe)

In my initial stages of growing up, my frame of thought for relationships sat a little *"to-the-left, to-the-left"*, like those catchy lyrics of Beyonce's song, Irreplaceable. Well at least that's the lie the devil tried to make me believe.

You see, Satan tried to convince me that my vibe was off. That I had a bad attitude and that's why I didn't have a whole slew of friends outside of my siblings and church social circle. The enemy tried to imprison me with the mentality that, I had "daddy issues." Trying to convince me with the lie that, "I wasn't whole because I was being raised by a single mom."

Satan came for my emotional well-being super early in my life's journey. Like before I knew there was such a mindset or heart-posture. Satan was trying to stop me from empowering you the way that God strengthen me to do.

That scripture that says, "the enemy comes to steal, kill, and destroy….", (John 10:10). That verse is the real deal.

You see, you are in full control of your mood and emotions, But if you're not careful, you'll fall prey to the idea that your life is ran by how you feel; instead of what you do. Let's discuss our feelings and how god's grace becomes a remedy for shifting our mood.

When I was a little girl, I wanted to be like my brother who seemed to attract people wherever he went. Or maybe like my little sister who seemed to come home from school with a new best friend every week. What was wrong with me? Why didn't I have a grip (a bunch) of friends like they had?

I had to be defective. Maybe I had a bad attitude. Or maybe I didn't smile enough when out in public. Whatever it was, it couldn't have been good. And that feeling bothered me throughout my childhood.

As I grew into a young adult, I called myself trying to do what I saw others around me doing. I wanted to fit in. I would show people that I was just like them. But God blocked it.

The truth that God revealed to me while writing this chapter is, when you have a call of influence over your life, the enemy will try his best to pervert your sensibilities before you reach your optimal level of influence. Let me stop before I go too deep, too fast. Let's get a few definitions and descriptions out the way.

Nowadays, people are always talking about their mood, their vibe, or vibrations they receive from others. But what does it really mean? More importantly, what does God say about your mood?

Let's define the word, **"Mood"**. Google dictionary defines the word "mood" as a noun or adjective. Let's take a look down below:

Google Dictionary definition:

> NOUN- a temporary state of mind or feeling. (example: "they appeared to be in a very good mood about something"

> ADJECTIVE- (especially for music) inducing or suggestive of a particular feeling or state of mind.

The table below is just a sample of alternative words you can use to define or identify your choice word to describe your mood. We'll use these descriptions of mood as a point of reference while discussing grace + gratitude in correlation with our mood.

"Alternative words use for "Mood":

Attitude	Desire	Humor	Response
Atmosphere	Disposition	Inclination	Soul
Aura	Emotion	Individuality	Spirit
Character	Feelings	Mind/Mindset	Temper/Temperament
Condition	Frame of Mind	Personality	Wish

My Story

Growing up I can recall three different situations where I realized that God was protecting me from turning into a negative person. And that guarded viewpoint that I had was a hedge of protection; not a curse from God, which was the picture the enemy tried to trick me into believing.

Scenario 1: "Elementary School Playground"

In elementary school, I, like most kids, loved recess time. I couldn't wait to go out to the handball or tether-ball courts and get my play on! Those were my favorite recess activities. 😊

While out for recess, I would always see a group of kids standing on the sidelines talking loudly and looking like they were having fun. But I was never invited over to the hangout section.

As a matter of fact, when I would try to go see what all the fuss was about, one of my handball partners would call me over to double team some opponents on the handball court; so, I had to go.

I never made it over to that group of kids hanging out. You'll know why later in this chapter.

Scenario 2: "Skating Rink"

The City was Cerritos California. The setting was Skate Depot, roller skating rink. The music was always bumpin'. The parking lot was jumpin', and the DJ had the jams on lock. Skate depot was the place to be every Monday for observed federal holidays and always on the weekends. Oh, how I loved to skate.

My mother would allow each of her children to bring one church friend with us, and the party was, On! As soon as I put my skates on, I jumped on the skating rink floor. Ready to warm up my legs and ankles, so when my songs began to play back-to-back, I could really get my groove on.

My number one skate partner was my cousin, Charnessia. We goofed around, laughed, and danced on skate wheels until the soles of our feet almost formed blisters. Lol!!! We really loved skating.

You would think that being there with my best friend would distract me from the shenanigans going on within the building, but it didn't. I still noticed that we were outsiders in the rink of loud music and fun.

Why wasn't the cute older boys talking to me? Why wasn't me and my cousin over on the sidelines exchanging numbers, like the other teens were doing. I'll expound further after this next scenario.

Scenario 3: "The Church Gossip-Cypher"-

Oooo Charnyce, you better tread lightly. You can't be talkin' about the church like that. Simmer down my friend, it'll be okay. This same example can be applied to school, work, or any other place where people gather. Trust me.

See, I was born and raised in church. So, I've witnessed a lot of gossip-circles in my church attending years. They're pretty much all the same. Sister or Brother so-and-so spreading lies, rumors, truth, and fairy tales about other church goers. But no one ever spilled their own tea.

Now me knowing that this was what the gossip cyphers were all about, didn't make me steer clear of me wanting to be "down", like the Brandy song. I still wanted to be in the circle sipping tea.

But somehow or some way; the chatter always seemed to stop when I greeted the group. It was like God had a sign on my forehead that read, "You leave her outta the drama." So, the gossip group would keep it cute around me.

I guess that was great because it hurts my feelings when people talk about other people. Especially if they're not friends with those who are the topic of conversation. It also makes me look at the one gossiping with the side-eye. But anyway, back to my point.

Let me tell how dope God is. The enemy thought he had me, but I got away!! Every time I tried to have an attitude about not being included in the gossip sessions, I wasn't privy to. The playground time the kids didn't invite me to. The skate party sidebar conversations I missed out on. God showed me the flipside to each scenario.

God revealed His shield of protection over my developing spirit. Then He took me to His word to confirm what He said. All this was done to help me get an understanding on why I had to guard my heart and pay attention to the influences around me.

God directed me to Proverbs, chapter 4:1-2,4-5, 6-9, 10-27; in the NIV (New International Version) translation. The chapter reads as such:

Grace & Gratitude

Proverbs 4 - "Wisdom is Supreme"

1. Listen, my sons, to a father's instruction; pay attention and gain understanding.
2. I give you sound learning, so do not forsake my teaching.
3. When I was a boy in my father's house, still tender, and an only child of my mother,
4. He taught me and said, "Lay hold of my words with all your heart; keep my commands and you will live.
5. Get wisdom, get understanding; do not forget my words or swerve from them.
6. Do not forsake wisdom, and she will protect you; love her, and she will watch over you.
7. Wisdom is supreme; therefore, get wisdom. Though it cost all you have, get understanding.
8. Esteem her, and she will exalt you; embrace her, and she will honor you.
9. She will set a garland of grace on your head and present you with a crown of splendor.
10. Listen, my son, accept what I say, and the years of your life will be many.
11. I guide you in the way of wisdom and lead you along straight paths.
12. When you walk, your steps will not be hampered; when you run, you will not stumble.
13. Hold on to instruction, do not let it go; guard it well, for it is your life.
14. Do not set foot on the path of the wicked or walk in the way of evil men.
15. Avoid it, do not travel to it; turn from it and go on your way.
16. For they cannot sleep till they do evil; they are robbed of slumber until they make someone fall.
17. They eat the bread of wickedness and drink the wine of violence.
18. The path of the righteous is like the first gleam of the dawn, shining ever brighter till the full light of day.

19. But the way of the wicked is like deep darkness; they do not know what makes them stumble.
20. My son, pay attention to what I say; listen closely to my words.
21. Do not let them out of your sight, keep them within your heart.
22. For they are life to those who find them and health to a man's whole body.
23. Above all else, guard your heart, for it is the wellspring of life.
24. Put away perversity from your mouth; keep corrupt talk from your lips.
25. Let your eyes look straight ahead, fix your gaze directly before you.
26. Make level paths for your feet and take only ways that are firm.
27. Do not swerve to the right or the left; keep your foot from evil.

In this passage of wisdom, a father is speaking to his son on how to carry himself throughout his life. The father explained that the son is to be wise and pay attention to everything around him. He tells the son that he needs to stay on the straight path and turn from unstable roads and situations.

The father also explained that if the son heeded his instructions and walked the road of wisdom, the son would make great sacrifice to gain wisdom. That wisdom would protect him, sustain him, and he (the son) would live a long prosperous life.

The father pointed out that the son should steer clear of evil. That some people would be placed in his path to make him stumble; and that was their only purpose.

God Vibes ....

Now let's revisit the different scenarios in which God shifted my mood and emotions.

Scenario 3- The enemy tried to make me feel like I was missing out on life because I wasn't sipping the gossip "tea" that my church friends spoke of, and I felt sad. I wanted to be included in the dirt that was being dished, right? WRONG!

God protected me from hearing the negativity that was being spoken about different people in the church, because that would have affected how I saw those people. And it would've also deterred me from growing as a developing leader in the church, ministry, and in Christ.

I realized that I didn't need to sip the gossip-tea. I needed to focus on forming relationships with the congregants in the church and building a deeper relationship with Jesus Christ.

Not being religious and messy. I was shielded from hearing the rumors of the church members and I was able to learn and grow at each and every church I've ever been a member of.

Scenario 2-

When I reflected on my socialization on the playground, I came to the realization that God placed a hedge of protection around me (Psalm 91). The Holy Spirit shielded me from the misfits that would have caused me to stumble in grade school.

Those kids were out there teaching each other curse words and play-fighting. Throwing insults and bullying one another.

Now you know I would have ended up on the principal's list as one of the bad kids that ended up being transferred to continuation school… lol! So, it's good that I wasn't invited to play with those kids.

Scenario 2-

As for the skate parties. Let me tell you how cool God is. God impressed upon my mother the take me, my siblings, and cousins to the skating rink on the holidays. So, I didn't miss out on the fun. I was just protected from the foolishness.

While Me and the fam-bam was on the skating floor learning and trying out new skate moves and tricks. The teens and young adults with ulterior motives were on the sideline drinking thunderbird, smoking cigarettes and weed, and some were even tipping into the bathrooms to have sex!

Now you know my "sweet-little-baby-Jesus" self, needed to stay on the skating floor practicing my skate moves instead of possibly going half on a baby on the sidelines. Thank You Jesus!

God-Moment:

What I came to realize is that aura that I thought was me having a bad attitude that caused me to miss out on acceptance and interaction from those different crowds; was actually; the Holy Spirit setting me apart from a wayward future.

I was shielded from falling into the bad-choices trap. My friends and I now call the bad-decision making phase- the "Young, dumb, and stupid phase", lol…

Had I been accepted into those crowds and begun engaging in the harmful and adult things that those kids and young adults were doing, I wouldn't have lived to see God blocking me from the gossip conversations with the church crew. Because my mama would have killed me after finding out I'd tried to smoke, drink, or have sex 😊, lol!!!

No, but for real, as a woman with an ever-evolving relationship with Jesus Christ today; I now understand that it's okay if I'm not always invited to the cookout or bonfire. I'll be okay if I don't make it to every birthday party or lounge celebration.

You see, God's grace ushers in the gift of wisdom to guide you. To teach you to be sensitive to the guidance of the Holy Spirit. The Holy Spirit then shows you who and what situations to steer clear of.

Now that You know God's grace is a whole vibe. I hope you can take the scripture passage in this chapter and apply it to your life.

You see, there's always a reason to thank and praise God. He is the ultimate Mood-Shifter. But you must want to be changed. Do you desire a mood-shift? If so, let's try it right here and now.

Prayer

Dear Heavenly Father. I'm not sure what parts about my outlook needs rearranging, but You know all. Lord, please search my heart. If there is anything not like You or not pleasing in Your sight; please take it out. Reveal those unfavorable things to me so that I can work on them. Thank You, God, for this word and approach to shifting my attitude. In Your mighty name I pray, Amen.

Exercise

Write a letter to your feelings/attitude. It doesn't matter if you currently hold this mindset because you're reading and exercising your right to change, this day. If you don't think there's anything wrong with your disposition, but those close to you have pointed out a few flaws… Let's write those things down. Now, as you go to God in prayer, this will be the time to give your old mindset to the Heavenly Father. Allow God to bless you with a new point of view.

Grace & Gratitude

Write Your
Grace + Mood = God Vibe

Grace & Gratitude

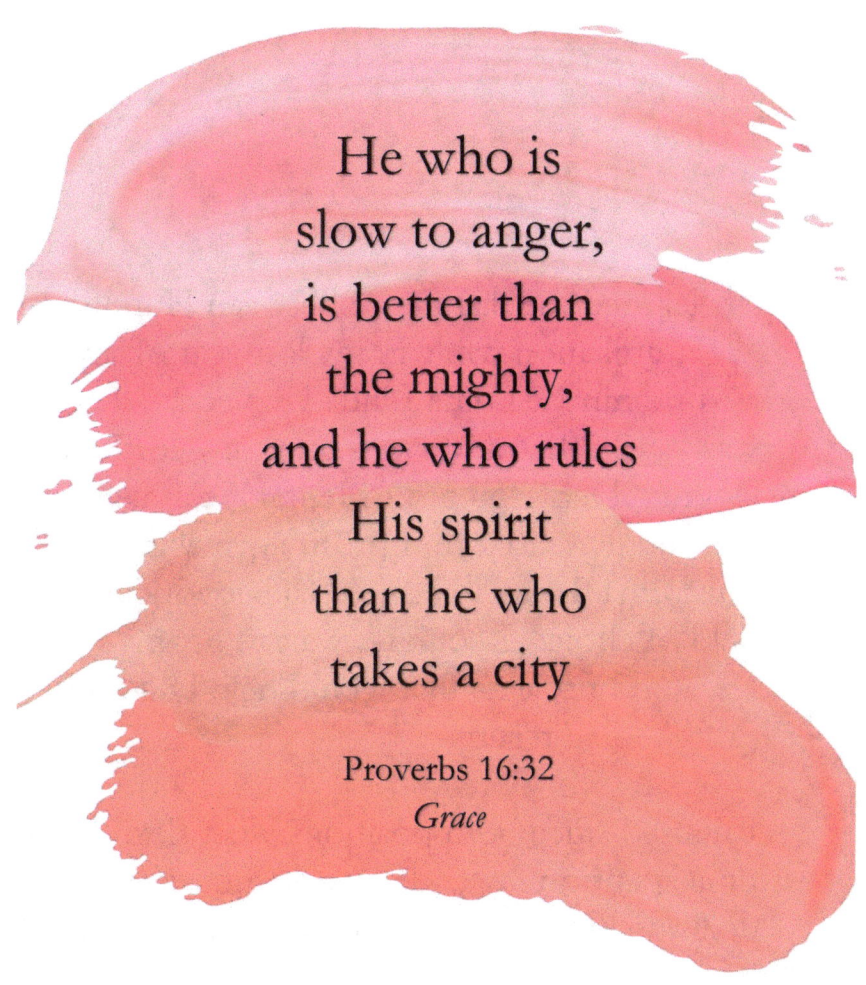

He who is
slow to anger,
is better than
the mighty,
and he who rules
His spirit
than he who
takes a city

Proverbs 16:32
Grace

Chapter 17
Humility vs. Humiliation

I learned the difference between Humility and Humiliation while in my last year of my master's program at Loma Linda University. The year was 2012-2013, and I was interning for Riverside County, Department of Mental Health; along with a community based non-profit agency in Loma Linda, California. I was so excited to be working in my field of choice. I couldn't wait to get my hands on a few good projects that would help build my professional resume.

I figured since both positions were flexible with time spent on my coursework and reserved hours dedicated to learning each job; I could easily do both.

Boy was I wrong! I didn't factor in that this would mean I would be working full-time hours, taking six graduate level courses; not to mention, nursing myself back to health after a bad lupus flare the year before.

When the school year first began, I had all the energy a girl could ask for. I had been bound to my house for an entire school year, rehabbing from a horrible bout with lupus, and my cabin fever was real! During my rehab time, I just kept asking God,

> "Father God, restore my health. Give me the strength to finish what I started with this graduate degree. My mind is ready to receive the information I need to be the best social service professional I can be! Lord, I'm ready. I can do this!"

I found myself giving my sales pitch of a clean bill of health to God, praying that He would agree it was time for me to get back to the rat-race of life.

I felt the pressure to get back into the swing of things even more because I'd received notice from the University that I only had one year of financial aid assistance left in my initial contract. So, I was really under the gun when it came to completing my last six classes, by the financial aid deadline.

Then there was the medicine I was taking. I know for sure the prescription steroids I was taking had me trippin', because this last year of school was going to be more than anyone should endure. I had convinced myself that I could do the impossible, I just had to stay focused.

I arrived at the Riverside County internship ready to roll. I had my Internship Coursework syllabus and laptop in tow. I was super focused with a smile on my face, and I was ready to face the school quarter head on! At least, that's what I thought initially.

During the student orientation at Riverside County, I was introduced to all the department managers and directors. Each director stated their name and a specific project they would like each intern to assist on.

After the orientation, I was assigned to work on a project to train county paraprofessionals on theoretical constructs from some of the most famous theorists in the Mental and Behavioral Health field.

I figured this would be a breeze. I was very familiar with the theories in the training manual. I had studied these same practices before, and I was comfortable with public speaking. This project was in the bag!

I didn't realize I had overcommitted myself. When the department director asked for my estimated timeline to be ready to present my first training course. I gave a start date of 30 days to learn how to present subject matter to a well-established group of county employees. I didn't even bat an eye.

I would learn the county's way of building a project and presenting for training employees, and Wala! I would be crowned "the next top intern" in the world of intern training programs, for the state of California! Wrong!!!

What ended up happening is that training project was actually much larger than what I was capable of accomplishing independently. I had spread myself too thin. Between my six course classes, my supervision hours, my two work-study intern jobs and lupus recovery treatment; I was all over the place.

I found myself becoming physically fatigued, couldn't eat, barely sleeping; and all because I was juggling too many things at one time. By the end of the school quarter, the project was shelved by the department director, and I was assigned to a lesser task. I was so embarrassed.

Why did I tell the managers and directors that I could take on such a big project in such a short amount of time? Not even the seasoned training managers could pull that time-frame off. What was I thinking?!!!

My internship supervisor pulled me into her office to discuss my next steps and plan for the remaining time in the program. I remember sitting down at the supervisor's desk and looking at the floor. I felt defeated and humiliated. I was beating myself up on the inside, and it was written all over my face.

Supervisor: "Charnyce, why such a long face? Tell me what's going on in that head of yours? You don't look like yourself. Where's that smile I'm used to seeing?
I raised my head to say what was on my mind.

Me: "I am so embarrassed. The training project was shelved indefinitely, and I didn't even get to complete the training modules. I feel stupid for taking on such a large project and not giving myself enough time to dissect the material so that I could deliver the information in a more clear and concise way. It's my fault the project was shelved! I'm so embarrassed."

After speaking my peace, I dropped my head again and began to cry. With tears dripping from my lashes, I explained to my supervisor that my school, work, and rehab schedules were running me ragged. I told her how I hadn't been getting any rest due to me having such a demanding course load and full-time work hours between both of my jobs.

I began sobbing even louder when I mentioned that I felt I had overcommitted myself for the school year, and I felt like I had no other choice but to see everything through.

My supervisor reached across her desk and placed her hand on top of mine. She then told me something that I knew God had delivered through her. She said to me,

> "Charnyce, you have to give yourself some grace. The master's program is probably one of the most demanding programs you will ever experience. I know a lot is being asked of you. But you must take a step back to see what's best for your health and well-being.
>
> That project that you were assigned to has been passed on several different times by the mental health department. So don't feel bad. You did what you could do. And you championed through a difficult task that many tenured employee trainers wouldn't have even attempted. You are going to be a great leader in the near future, Charnyce. Keep your head up."

Before the meeting was over, my supervisor said that she wanted me to focus on some self-care exercises because she noticed my lack of energy and usual sluggish demeanor.

God also shifted the atmosphere in the department, where I was able to slow down my thinking and devise a plan of action that would help me get through the rest of the school year.

I got together with the students from my cohort, and we developed study manuals to help one another consume all the required reading that we had. And I was able to go to my rheumatology appointments and treatment sessions, during my personal time.

Self-Reflective Moment:

I believe because I was willing to be transparent and humble before my supervisor, she was able to affirm me and assist me with my struggles. Then God took it a step further and paired me with a student cohort that was supportive and truly cohesive. So, it all worked out for my good.

No one tried to embarrass or humiliate me. They would literally ask me if I needed anything. And I humbly asked for and accepted the help.

Don't be afraid to speak up when the waters of your life seem to be rising above where you can swim. Call on the Holy Spirit. His grace is sufficient (2 Corinthians 12:9)

Prayer

Dear God, help me to know when I need to call on You. I want to rest and abide in Your grace and mercy. Cast out any prideful deeds or thoughts that would cause me to not walk in humility. Humiliation is the work of the enemy that discourages me from walking boldly in the call You have on my life. Lord, I thank you for your grace, Amen.

Exercise

Now take a moment to write 3 experiences in your life where you experienced Humility or Humiliation.

Grace & Gratitude

Write That Thang Out!

I will make all My
goodness pass before you,
and I will proclaim the
name of the Lord
before you.
I will be gracious to whom
I will be gracious,
and I will have compassion
on whom I will have
compassion.

Exodus 33:19
Grace

Chapter 18
Grace and the Soul-Tie Trap

The year was 1999 and I graduated from high school and attended Long Beach State University in Southern California. The rapper, Juvenile's "Back that thang up" hit the air waves, and all you can hear every time you turned on the radio is, "Girl you look good, won't ya back that thang up!".

I think that was the first time I'd ever seen women twerkin'. Except, back then; we called the move, backin' that thang up, like the song.

That year was such a magical time for me. I was now 18 years old, a college student. I had my own car, financial aid, in the bank. I was cute-in-the face and slim in the waist.

Everything was everything as my uncle's junior and Wimpy use to say. I thought life couldn't get any better.

Then on New Years Eve night, at Club Metro in Riverside, California; I met him.
He was 5" 11", and 180 pounds of chocolatey goodness.

Smooth dark chocolate skin, check.
Pearly white teeth, check.
Muscles from head-to-toe, check
Broad shoulders… check, check.

This dude was gorgeous.
Now, I'm not a woman who loves chocolate candy; however, I do love me a chocolate skinned man. God bless my America for the chocolate dudes of the world, Ting 😊! lol!!!

On top of all that, this guy had a military high-fade haircut. And the blend was perfect. Me coming from a family of hairstylists, I noticed his fade right away. This was my kinda guy.

When we caught each other's eye, it seemed like no one else was in the club. The club was dimly lit above our heads, but I could still see his smile. Ole' boys' dental work was poppin'.

Military-Bae walked up to me and asked me to dance. He was a whole vibe. But being the self-proclaimed playa that I was, I played it cool and placed my hand in his. He pulled me close as we began to groove to the bumpin' beats the DJ was spinning. Every song after our introduction seemed like my new favorite song. I was lost in his groove and loving every bit of it.

Between his cologne and his southern accent, as he whispered in my ear; I was on cloud nine. We danced all night until the last call for alcohol was shouted over the speakers.
Everyone knew the club was closing because the DJ played, "T-Shirt and my Panties", by Adina Howard.

So, if you were trying to make your hook up happen before the guys and girls started their "parking-lot-pimpin'", you better get that number before you walk out the door.

The building lights came on and we adjusted our gaze at one another. His face matched his handsome smile, and I knew he was gonna be my next boyfriend. We exchanged numbers, and he told me he'd call me before he went to bed.

He explained that he and his friends had driven down from the Marine base in Joshua Tree, and he wanted to know if he could come see me the next day.

He was my type, my size, the right height, and weight. So, you know I said, Yes.

My friends were calling me to come get in the car so we could go get something to eat. Marine-Boo lipped "bye Niecye".
I turned around and smiled. Then I jumped in the car with the party-crew to head to Denny's for some after-the-club food and recap of the night.

The club recap with the party-crew was always fun. There were guys and girls. We sat around the restaurant table chatting and laughing about our favorite parts of the night.

The tailgate to a nearby eatery kept the mackin' session going. However, this night was different. I did meet a couple of cuties while I was ringing in the new year, but Military-Bae was the dude I had my sights set on.

Each person at the table took the numbers out of their pockets. We like to see who'd collected the most numbers by the end of the night. That person would have the bragging rights until the next outing.

Even though I collected a great deal of numbers that night, Military-Bae stood out. I must have checked my pager every 30 minutes until I went home.

The time was 2:00 a.m., and I had just made it to my parent's house in time for their curfew. As I kicked my shoes off and started to undress, I see my beepers vibrating as it danced across my nightstand. It was the dude from the military area code.

He was from Alabama, so his number would display a "205" area code. I smiled as I reached for the cordless phone on my nightstand. He kept his word and paged me. I didn't waste any time returning his call.

That first phone conversation was like most honeymoon phase conversations. It was a few hours long, with him and I asking surface questions and giving basic answers. We were both 18, fresh out of high school.

I was attending college, and he had enlisted in the military. Neither of us had been in love before, but I had a good feeling that it wouldn't be our story for too much longer.

We met up the next day for lunch and the chemistry was undeniable. We laughed and talked for hours until his boys' dates with their girls' time had come. I didn't want the hangout to end, but I knew we didn't have forever.

So, I got up from the restaurant table and stretched out my arms for a hug.
He took hold of my hand and pulled me into his arms. Then he whispered in my ear, "I miss you already, Niecye P.".

My body flushed with warm tingly feelings. As I lifted my head from his chest, we looked into each other's eyes, and it happened. He kissed me like he loved me.

Well, kinda like a "like-love" kinda kiss.

That type of kiss where you don't really know the person enough to love them, but the: attraction + the chemistry + "Oooo, I think I like him" vibe is there.

It was magical. At that moment, I knew this is what the start of loving someone felt like. I wiggled out of his embrace because that strong connection made me a bit nervous. I stepped back to gather myself and smile. We looked at each other and knew we were definitely liking-on one another.

I got in my car and put on my seat belt. He asked me to roll down my window. Then he leaned in and kissed me again. This time the kiss was even more intense. And as I began kissing him back, I felt it… The beginning of our soul tie.

We sent beeper codes all day that day. I was smitten. This guy would surely be my man, going into this new year.

Before he left to go back to the Marine base, I already knew I had fallen for him. The way he looked at me. The way he talked to me. The way he held my hand and hugged me when it was time for him to leave.

He didn't care that his boys were teasing him for spending the entire weekend with me.

I guess he was supposed to be juggling girls like they were. Whatever their initial plan was, he and I were laser focused on one another.

Every day after that weekend, we were in communication with each other. We spoke on the phone each morning and every night. And the weekends!?!... the convo's doubled up. It was like that, "fall asleep on the phone kinda love". Y'all know how that 1st love thang be.

Valentine's Day, My birthday, any random day. He sent gifts and flowers. I ran up my phone bill talking to him before cell phone and land line minutes were free. He paid the phone bill. That made me fall even deeper in love with him. I was in "lovalicious: with him.

Christmas 2000 rolled around, and we had been on cloud nine all year long. "Military Boo" had flown out to spend Christmas with me and my family. He fit right in. Then he "flewed" me out to North Carolina where he was stationed.

We drove to Alabama, for him to introduce me to his family. Everyone was nice and hospitable. It seemed like a match made in heaven. I couldn't get enough of this man.

New Year's Day 2001 came, and all was still well on lover's lane. He would fly to come see me. Or I would fly to see him. Then life got real.

The tower bombing of 9/11 happened. He was deployed for 9 months. I wasn't familiar with the military culture, so I had no idea how deployment worked. Even better, I didn't imagine how the two of us being away from each other without daily communication would affect our relationship.

I thought he would be sent abroad, and I would still be able to keep in contact with him like we had been for the past year. We spoke when he first arrived to the destination, and I was cool with that.

Then the calls, emails and conversations became fewer and far between. Until one day, there was no contact at all. By this point I was sick-with-it (sick to my stomach). I didn't know if he was alive, injured, avoiding me, or dead-

Then one day, out of the blue; he called me. The guilt in his voice had me shook. I knew something wasn't right. He started the conversation off with a weak apology. I say "weak" now, but I bought into it hook-line-and-sinker back then 😊.

He first apologized for not calling me. He said he felt bad because he knew that what he'd done was wrong and he didn't know how he would tell me. He went on to say that he'd been hanging out and sleeping with a female marine on base. I was devastated.

He then began to ask me how I was feeling… I was a little confused at the question. Physically, I felt fine.

So, then he took a long pause and said, "You should go get tested. This hoe say she got a STD. And me and you made love before I left. So, you could have it too."

I was upset but mostly hurt. If I could have reached through the phone and knocked him upside his head. I would have. I told him that I would call him back when I had the test results. Then I hung up.

How could this be happening to me? I'd been in a committed relationship for over a year. I loved him and he said he loved me too! He even gave me a half karat diamond ring as a promise for us to get married one day. WE were meant to be! I just couldn't believe it.

When the test results came back, the doctor requested that I come to the medical office to receive the results. I thought to myself, that couldn't be good news. My thoughts were accurate. He had given me an STD.

I was pissed! I waited a week to call him. I didn't have the words. Now I'm taking these antibiotics and drinking water like a fish, because of this dude's selfishness. I was so wide open for this dude. He was the love of my life. Why would he cheat on me?

He disappeared for another few weeks. Not so much as a smoke signal to let me know he was okay. I was heartbroken and furious at the same dang time. I thought to myself. How dare he cheat on me and then disappear with no word.

I was so embarrassed. I beat myself up for having sex with him before marriage. I told myself that it was okay because he was going to be my husband one day.

Well, this wasn't going to be that day. And based on this STD situation, I would have gone on with being treated. I could've ended up not being able to have children in the future.

We took a long break from each other after that. I focused on college and doing hair on the weekends. During that stretch of a few years, God began calling me. I began dreaming dreams of children being born.

My oldest sister and a few of the older teens at my grandparents' church were starting to get married and have kids. And here I was wondering when my time for a lasting love would come.

The entire time we stayed out of contact with each other; I beat myself up. How could I let myself fall in love with this dude? He wasn't even from Cali! It was unrealistic to think that relationship could actually work.

On top of all that, I had sex with this cat, and didn't even think to use protection. I gave him my body without even thinking if he could have a disease. I felt horrible and looked like a fool. I beat myself for years.

I stopped wearing the promise ring he bought me. I placed that thang right in the ring box and didn't think about it anymore. When friends or family asked how we were doing. I would lie and say, we agreed to take a break.

The relationship with this Military-Bae was off and on for so many years that I was ashamed after a while to admit that I was still dealing with him. He would come to Cali and get a hotel room, and there I was laid-up with him again. Going out on dates again.

Accepting his lies and gifts, again. Each time I took him back, he disrespected and neglected me; and we broke up, again- The merry-go-round of relationship lasted from 18 to 25 years old. But this time, he'd remixed his lie a little bit. I feel for it hook, line and sinker.

The phone call went a little something like this:

> Military-Dude, "Hi beautiful, can I talk to you for a moment".
>
> Me rolling my eyes with my bible on my lap sitting in my North Hollywood apartment that I shared with my little sister.
>
> Me, "Yeah, what's up. What's poppin'?"
>
> Military-Dude, "I want to come see you. I want to talk face to face."

I agreed to let him come visit me in Cali, and I was **back in the soul-tie-trap, yet again…**

Grace & Gratitude

He flew into Cali the next week, and as soon as he walked out the gate, I knew I was in trouble. Time had done his body good! You hear me. He was even sexier than what I'd remembered the years before. Except this time, he was older, more experienced, and even more cunning. 😈

My inner church-girl was bracing herself for impact because I knew the devil had landed. My Holy-Spirit-light, that flamed in my heart was flashing the caution sign. But I chose to ignore it. I was nervous this time around. But that didn't stop me from opening myself up to this man again. I still listened to what he had to say.

> **Military-Dude-** "Thank you for letting me come to visit you. I know it took a lot for you to let me back into your life. I wanted let you know that I've changed. I'm out of the military now. I have a high-paying position in Alabama, and I want you to be my lady."

I must have looked like a deer caught in the headlights because I just sat there with my mouth shut and my eyes wide open. I shook off the initial shock and replied,

"Why the sudden change of heart? We haven't spoken to each other in years. Now here you are asking me to come live with you in Alabama?"

Military-Dude - "I know it sounds crazy, but I've loved you ever since we were 18 years old. I'm in love with you, Charnyce. And I didn't know how much I appreciated you until I sat back one day and realized you were no longer in my life. You're the love of my life Charnyce. I want you to be my wife and I want to take care of you."

I fell for his words once again. This time he had upped the ante. He showed me his salary from his new job and his latest bank statement. He told me that he'd been saving up his money to move me to Alabama. He was serious about us, and he wanted to meet with my mom and stepdad to ask for my hand in marriage.

Long story short, I believed him and ended up moving to Alabama six months after he'd popped back up out of thin air.

The initial move was quick, but something didn't feel quite right. I immediately started looking for schools to enroll in. If he wanted to take care of me financially, I would at least go back to school and get another degree. Ya girl has always been goal-oriented. But first I would have to make sure we tied-that-knot. I would not be living-in-sin in Alabama. No sir-ree!

Six months had passed, and we still weren't married. My graduate school application was denied, and I was starting not to feel so well. Military-Bae had been spending more and more time at work. So, I was just in the apartment by my lonesome. Wasting away. I'd lost weight from not eating.

I wasn't trying to starve myself. I just didn't have much of an appetite. I was feeling sad and isolated. At this point I needed to go back home to Cali.

Then all of a sudden, I woke up one day barely able to breathe or lift my head off of the pillow. I was sick as a dog, and I needed Military-Bae to come home from work and take me to the hospital.

As I called and texted him back-to-back. I begin to feel this pain in my chest. Then my breathing became shallow. I really needed to see a doctor- quick, fast, and in a hurry.

By the time he arrived home that night, I was emotional and barely able to catch my breath. I couldn't even cuss him out like I wanted to because I was too weak, and my chest was hurting like crazy!!! So, I simply demanded he take me to the nearest emergency room.

Next thing I knew, I woke up lying in a hospital bed with an IV in my arm and two different bags of medication running through the machine.

What had I done to myself?

How did I end up in the hospital in Montgomery, Alabama. This couldn't be what God had for me....

The Holy Spirit came to me and said:

"It's time to go home, Charnyce ..."

I couldn't go back to Cali this time. Could I? He said he loved me. He asked my parents' for my hand in marriage. He even showed us his bank statements. And anybody who knows me knows that I'm for real about money.

I was so head-over-heels for this man that I would do anything for him. Including packing all my belongings, leaving my good job with benefits, and leaving my covering in California.

This move had to work. Right?

Wrong!...

While trying to settle into this new life I learned that ole boy was up to his same old tricks.

As I laid in the hospital with excruciating chest pains; I started to realize that I'd made a big mistake. The chest pains were worsening by the hour. My heart felt like a body builder reached in my chest, grabbed my heart and was squeezing it tight.

When the doctors came in for their rounds, I was shocked to hear what my test results were. I was told I had yet another STD and a UTI, which I knew he had so generously gifted me.

Here I was again, following his "little-big-head" down south instead of yielding to the caution sign that the Holy Spirit kept showing me in visions and dreams. My body was exhausted, and my heartbroken. I was now embarrassed and angry.

By this point, I was angrier with myself than Miliary-Fiancé. I was in the hospital for a whole week and all I could hear in my head was the lyrics to the hymn,

    Love lifted me ….

> "I was sinking deep in sin
> Far from the peaceful shore
> Very deeply stained within
> Sinking to rise no more.
> But the Master of the sea
> Heard my despairing cry
> From the waters lifted me
> Now safe am I."

Grace & Gratitude

Every day that I sat in the hospital my desire to get back to my family grew stronger and stronger. However, when Bae would call and talk to me, that dang soul-tie-trap wrapped itself around my heart like a noose. Squeezing out the very common sense that I had left.

I found myself torn between what my head knew would be best for me and what my heart wanted. I wanted to please my fiancé, but I needed to see-about myself even more.

The crazy part was, I was in the hospital for an entire week, and he never came to sit with me. 😔

By the time he finally came to check on me, my heart and head was at war within me.
However, I had made up my mind that I would follow my head and go back to Cali to be with my covering.

I told the doctors I just needed to be stable enough to fly home to California. I had made up in my mind that being with my family and friends was more important than being married to him.

Going home was more important than explaining to everyone why I moved back home.

More important than trying to make up a lie to say why I wasn't ever going back to Alabama.

But the struggle was real …

The sight of him made my stomach and heart ache at the same dang time. I felt like I was Peter from the bible in Matthew 14:22-33. It's the chapter where Jesus walked on water and asked that Peter join Him. Peter was afraid and said that he couldn't do it because he was afraid, he'd drown.

I was so "Torn'" like the Letoya Luckett's song. I was in love with this dude, and I wanted to become his wife. But then here was God calling me to step out into the water that would lead me back to safety. Back to a healthier body and life.

The feeling of embarrassment washed over me as I just kept singing "Love Lifted Me".

Laying in that hospital bed the day before I was set to leave the hospital, my heart started to break. Internally I was beating myself up again.

"Girl, you gotta get yourself together. This guy doesn't love you; God does.

This dude got you in the hospital in another state, with no one here to sit with you. God has never left you. You have to go home."

The Holy Spirit countered the thought, with Deuteronomy 31:6; reminding me that God has never left me or forgotten about me.

The next day Military-Bae came to pick me up, and to my surprise he had his grandmother with him. He said she'd asked him to bring her to visit me.

Struggling to sit up straight in the bed and hug his grandmother, she hurried to my side. She told me to rest and asked her grandson to give us some time alone. The moment his feet exited the doorway I began to cry. I tried to show a brave face, but I knew I needed to go back home to Cali.

His Grandma, "Oh baby, you don't look so good. How you feelin?"

Me: "I'm jacked up grandma, I told the doctors if they can just get me strong enough to fly, I'm gonna go back to California."

His grandma touched my shoulder and said, *"It's time for you to go home sweetie."*

Our eyes settled on each other, and I reached my hands out to gesture for a hug. His grandma hugged me tightly. I knew at that moment; I would never see her again.

On the plane ride home, my body was trembling. All I could think about was how my ex wasn't there for me in my time of need. I harbored some serious hatred for him thinking about all the years of lies, cheating and deceit I'd experienced through being tied to him.

But worse than that; I was beating myself up even more. No one needed to say, "I told you so…". Or anything along those lines because my inner self recited those words to myself every day for years. Then one day, God healed my unforgiving heart towards myself and my ex. The hatred that I had for ole boy was gone.

Grace & Gratitude

I always said he was my first real love relationship. But, in actuality; God is my first love. I had abandoned my bond with God for a fraud.

The hate and anger I had for my ex was trying to ruin my future ability to love again. But God's grace was always there.

The Heavenly Father placed those memories deep down in the back of my subconscious, so that I might be able to forge new love relationships later in life.

The shame that I'd felt for years for chasing this selfish excuse for love, redeemed by Grace. You see, God performed spiritual heart surgery on me where my heart had been tattered, used up, and taken for granted. HE replaced it with His healing power of Grace.

I am now renewed and restored. So, I ask you now, if God's grace vindicated me; what miracle could His grace do for you?

Grace & Gratitude

The Holy Spirit had to help me reclaim my heart. I had to go and take back my peace by rebuilding my relationship with the Heavenly Father. I had to forgive my ex for all he had done. Most importantly, I had to forgive myself.

In 2013, Tasha Cobbs-Leonard released her debut music project called **Grace**. When I tell you this album blessed me! Chile! Chile! I still praise God every time I hear songs from the Grace project. One song that sticks to my soul is "Grace Saved Me".

God's grace literally mended the broken pieces of my heart and comforted me every time I began beating myself up, emotionally. God reminded me that He would heal my broken heart. He had forgiven me for ignoring the Holy Spirit's warnings; and that I was redeemed.

What I know for sure is that God is no respecter of persons. If He'll do it for me, He'll do it for you too. Now let's go the God in prayer.

Prayer

Dear Father God, I come to you broken. In need of more than I probably could even name or know to ask for. I ask that You come into my heart and breathe life where there's been damage, death, and disappointment.

Create in me a clean heart and renew a right spirit in me (Psalm 51:10-19). Please restore my joy and strength in You, that I may be able to live again.

 Help me to forgive the people in my life that have hurt me. And I pray that I will be forgiven as well. Help me to stop kicking myself when I am at an emotionally low place. Help me to show love through Your grace.

Lastly, I ask Father, that You break the yoke of the soul-tie-traps that I've entertained in my life. Help me to replace those connections with a deeper relationship with You. In Your mighty name I pray, Amen!

Exercise

Grab a piece of paper. Draw 4 columns on the page. On each column of the paper, write down: your name, God, and the names of the people that have done harm to you. Lastly, the people that you know you've done harm to. Ask the Heavenly Father for forgiveness.

Then ask God how He would like to use this list of people in your life to assist you in applying grace. Ask the Father to reveal which connections are soul-tie-traps and help you to break the yoke. Allow God's grace to find you, like it found me.

Grace & Gratitude

Get these Emotions & Thoughts Outside of Me!

My grace is sufficient for you, for My power is made perfect in your weakness; therefore, I will boast all the more gladly about my weaknesses, so that Christ's power may rest on me.

2 Corinthians 12:9 (ESV)
Grace

Chapter 19
A Conversation with Grandma Joyce
(Gratitude)

There are so many things that I am grateful for today. Surprisingly, I give thanks for both good and bad experiences. Words of encouragement, criticism (or what I like to call- "constructive encouragement"); and even those who doubt me.

Truth be told, there was a time in my life when I was super prideful as a child. I wouldn't apologize for anything. I would get a pop on the thigh or a swat on my butt because I wouldn't say "excuse me." Nor would I say, "Thank you."

How can a person so small have the mentality that people owed them anything? I spent a great deal of time with my grandma Joyce, back then. When my grandma noticed these character flaws, she offered up some words of wisdom.

I couldn't remember if we were at her house prepping food for one of the many meals she cooked throughout each day; or if we were at the beauty salon pricing and stocking inventory. All I know is that her words stuck to my bones like the collard greens and homemade biscuits that she could make with her eyes closed.

My grandma said to me, "Baby, the world don't owe you nuthin'. As a matter of fact, your parents are only responsible for getting you to age eighteen. Then you do the rest. Do you know that?"

I looked at my grandma stunned as if she'd cursed me out, lol... I thought for sure that the world owed me everything. Or at least my parents did. They're the ones who created me.

Then she explained, "Baby, God gives you the gift of life. And He uses your mama and daddy as the vessels to bring you into this world. When you come out your mama's womb, HE (God) breathes the breath of life into you that day; and every day after that. You see, every day is not promised to you.

Grace & Gratitude

So, you have to do the best with what you got. Then one day, hopefully, God will call you on home to be with Him.

That's just the cycle of life. You gotta be grateful for the time spent here on earth. And you need to make good of your time. Now you should want to please God. But it's all up to you."

I loved to listen to my grandma because she had such a wealth of knowledge that I could glean from. Even before I knew what "gleaning" was. Her nuggets of wisdom were like gems that you could cash in when you were ready to level-up.

My grandma continued….

> "You see, I grew up poor. I was 16 years old when mama died. My mama was shot by my stepdaddy and left fa' dead. Me and my younger sisters had to go stay with daddy. But He was on the road for work, so I had to look after me and my sisters.

By the time I saw my stepfather last, I was an adult with kids of my own. So, you see the world don't owe you nuthin' baby. Not even if you grow up with ya parents.

If ya' parents are alive, go see about em'. If you know there is a God, tell him Thank You for bringing you in the world. When your life comes to its end you can only hope to hear God say, "Well done thy good and faithful servant," (Matthew 25:23).

Now, as a full fledge adult, this message from my grandma is hitting me like a ton of bricks. In this chapter I want you to turn your attention on how to own your contributions to your personal life's development.

I'm sure you have come across a few people who have asked you what you were grateful for. Maybe you've asked yourself. However, the topic has presented itself, I just want to know, have you stopped to thank God. Have you said Thank you Lord for getting you to the place you've reached in your life right now?

My grandma was a loving and giving person. When she could have been cold and selfish; but she chose different. She chose to thank God for all that He had done for her in her life, instead of focusing on the negative. She had that Psalm 34 theme of gratitude all over her.

And she was blessed gorgeously for her gratitude. Her later years were far better than her former years. And all the life lessons that she was able to share with me and anyone else that dared to listen, was a process.

I encourage you to envision the people in your life who've introduced the concept of gratitude to you. Have you employed the practice? Take a moment to open your heart and mind up to a practice of gratitude.

Prayer

Dear Heavenly Father, I thank You that You breathed the breath of life into me every day. I've been granted the time and opportunity to reflect on all the many blessings large and small that have come into my life. Thank you for the opportunity to encounter people who has the patience and compassion to show and teach me the art of thanksgiving. In Your name I pray, Amen.

Exercise

List some people, stages in life, and experiences that you are grateful for. It might help to list where God has brought you from, and what your life looks like today.

Jot Down Your Grace Lesson

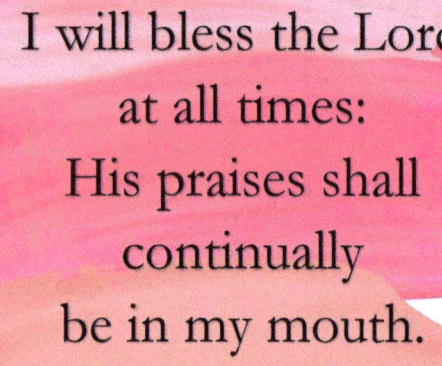

I will bless the Lord
at all times:
His praises shall
continually
be in my mouth.

Psalm 34:1
Gratitude

Chapter 20
The Covenant of Grace

If you haven't had the opportunity to view my videos on social media, then you haven't heard me talk about **Covenants** (relationships). If someone I know gave you this book, take a few seconds and go on Facebook or Instagram and look me up:

Charnyce Everythings New Perdue. Shameless plug.

I had one of my best female friends, Latoya (Toya) on the broadcast with me. The subject matter highlighted, "Good" and seemingly "Bad Blessings." I call Bad Blessings, "Blessings in Disguise."

I spoke about how your covenants help to guide you through identifying whether you're dealing with blessings or distractions. But enough about that video, let's focus on covenants.

According to Google dictionary, a covenant is described as,

> "*noun*
> an agreement.
>
> "There was a covenant between them that her name was never to be mentioned."
>
> **Similar:**
>
> Contract, compact, treaty, pact, accord, deal. Bargain, settlement, concordat protocol, entente agreement, arrangement, understanding, pledge, promise, bond, indenture, guarantee, commitment.
>
> *Verb*
> agree by lease, deed, or another legal contract.

Example- "The landlord covenants to repair the property."

Similar:

pledge, promise, agree, contract.

Toya and I's relationship falls under the Matthew 18:20 NKJV covenant. To be honest, all my God ordained relationships fall under the Matthew 18:20 blessing. Let's see what the scripture says,

> "For where two or three are gathered together in My name, I am there in the midst of them."

Now in the New King James translation of the bible, when Jesus is speaking, the words show up in red. So now you know this was the Savior speaking.

Back to my video….

During the recording, Toya and I spoke about different instances we'd had together where God was all up and through our mix. Like us having a "girls' day out."

We came together on this blessed Tuesday! There was shopping, lunching, and even a movie. Of course, this was prior to the pandemic. Because you WILL NOT catch me in too many outdoor activities right now. NO Ma'am, lol!...

It was as if Jesus Christ, the Holy Spirit, and God the Father was walking with us all day. We received bargains while shopping. Our meals were discounted to the point that they were almost $0.00. Then to top it all off, the movie tickets were FREE!!! Yes, I said it- Free!

Let me tell you… I was so shocked I was frozen in a slight trans to the point that Toya had to close my mouth, put my wallet back in my handbag and grab my hand to walk me into the movie theater.

What is so beautiful about our coming together is every single time we come together, our days go like that. If you have that kind of experience with a person every time the two of you come together, that's a sign of God's grace dripping all over that thang!

Grace & Gratitude

As far as me and Toya's covenant goes ...

When we're together- we are in sync. We discuss and pray over our individual lives and circumstances. We talk about our victories, desires, and fears. Even when we don't agree with one another, there is understanding and respect for one another's' feelings or opinion. We support each other and have a clear understanding of who each other are as individuals.

You see, God is not the author of confusion (1 Corinthians 14:33). When you connect to certain people, no matter the social setting; God is with you. And when His grace is on that union, there is peace, ease, compassion, and understanding in the equation.

God has blessed me with some great relationships. I spoke earlier about my mom and her parents. However, God is so dope; He will even bless you with people outside of your bloodline.

For me, I have my best male friend Ricco, Brother-in-law Kenny, mentor Bishop Anthony Richardson and my Bopsie-Twin Charnessia, and my uncle Kenny Perdue.

Now, these are just a few people that I speak to often; but my community of support is large. With each relationship I've listed there is accountability and grace.

My relationship with Ricco is so cool because he offers the male-perspective on different issues that we discuss. Topics like dating, male and female perspective, gender roles, responsibilities, and so on and so forth.

We often bounce ideas and viewpoints off each other frequently. And we serve as sounding boards for one another. And just in case I find myself in a situation that requires me to scream an obscene word, he does it for me, lol. I gave up cursing, so he has my back when I can't express myself, any other way 😉.

There's my brother-in-love, Kenny. We're one year apart in age and we act more like blood siblings. When I need a married-male point of view, he's there for me. I can confide in him, and it's not shared with anyone else.

Grace & Gratitude

Even when we need to lighten the mood of the conversation, we can share our love for 90's R&B music. And Bro-Bro, I haven't forgotten about us going to a New Edition concert in the future.

One of my spiritual mentors, Bishop Anthony Richardson; it's the "realness" for me! This man has a no-nonsense approach to life that speaks to the "Point-blank-periodt" part of my personality.

He reels me in when my words or actions don't align with the word of God, or my thoughts and actions don't serve me well. Bishop Anthony will get on my level and then tell me what God says about the matter. You gotta love that kind of communication.

I can't leave out my uncle Kenny Perdue. Yes, my bio-dad's brother. He is so cool. He's also a paster 😉. My Uncle Kenny serves as another voice of reason. He provides compassion, guidance, wisdom, practicality, and so much more. This man is truly an earthly angel for me.

In every different relationship or covenant I'm connected to, God assigned people to me for every aspect of my life. What I love most about my covenants is that, just like my Heavenly Father; my relationships never throw things up in my face.

There's never a "I told you so" or "Why you do that Charnyce?" There's just consistent reminders of who I am and who God has called me to be.

If God can bless me with covenant relationships like the connections I mentioned above, I am certain that He has or will do the same for you. God is not a respecter of person (Acts 10:28; Romans 2:11-16). He doesn't have favorites.

So, if You can't see the covenant relationships in your life, ask God to reveal them to you. If you are in need of a few good people to serve as confidants and sounding boards for you, ask the Heavenly Father to identify and send people to you.

The bible says, if you delight in the Lord, He will give you the desires of your heart (Psalm 37:4). God blesses the covenants He predestined for your life. Now let's go to God in prayer.

Grace & Gratitude

Prayer

Dear Heavenly Father, I come to You asking You to show me all the graceful covenants in my life. Any relationships that are not of You, take it away from me. Help me to identify all situations and circumstances that encompass Your presence. I thank You for the current and future relationships that You have instore for me. In Your name I pray, Amen.

Example

Now it's time for you to list your covenant connections that God has graced you with. Don't be discouraged. If you don't have a lot of covenants, God is always with you. And if you need someone, the bible says, "Ask and you will receive," (Matthew 7:7). Describe each relationship and how the connection aligns with God's heart for you. Can you see the presence of God in the relationship?

My Covenants = God Approved?... Yes, or No?

Grace & Gratitude

He said,
"My grace is
sufficient for
you,
For My strength
is
Made perfect
In weakness"

2 Corinthians 12:9
Grace

Chapter 21
God's Grace to Pivot!

Anyone who is living in this day and time has been affected by the pandemic. Those of us who are self-employed or deemed non-essential workers suffered major losses at the hands of the mandatory country-wide shut down. Me being from the large state of California, our governor declared a mandatory "stay-at-home" order for all non-essential workers or industries.

Us non-essential workers were forced to close down our businesses and wait for further instructions from the authorities. Well, my wait as a licensed Cosmetologist was approximately 8 to 9 months.

An interesting action I witnessed people do while waiting for clearance to return to work was, **"Pivot."** Now you may be thinking, Charnyce, what in the world does pivoting have to do with surviving, or thriving during these perilous times? Check this out.

You might not have been able to stop yourself from losing material things like jobs, houses, cars, and the ability to buy goods and services. But guess what!?! You made it through the uncertain times of the pandemic.

You see, God provided time and space for the world to sit still long enough to show us some, if not most of the giftings He's placed inside of us.

The truth of the matter is that you possess so many gifts that were placed into the fabric of your DNA by God, that all you truly need is the time, knowledge of your gifts and the opportunity to bring those things outside of you.

The pandemic granted you the opportunity to think about other ways you could spend your time or make a living caring for yourself and the people in your life.

Sitting still long enough for God to reveal those gifts to you; HE is more than able to help you take your next step into your destiny.

It's the "Pivot" for me!!!

Let's give you an example of what pivoting looks like. The word Pivot can translate differently in various settings. In the game of basketball, when a player is trying to protect the ball while figuring out whether to take the shot or pass the ball; they pivot. The dictionary defines the move as,

> "the action of rotating or turning on one foot while protecting your possession." In this case, you would be protecting the basketball.

Let's take this definition and example and apply it to your life. If you allow God to help you develop in your pivot, then you're able to plant your feet and trust in HIM to show you where to go and what to do. God will reveal to you your purpose, your gifts, and the plan He has for your life (Jeremiah 29:11, NKJV).

In the Holy Bible, there was a passage that spoke of a wither fig tree. Once you begin planting your feet in the presence of God, He is able to show you all the possibilities He's placed inside of you. He can also assist you in activating your faith in Him during the process.

It's the Pivot for Me!!!

My Story-

Before the pandemic, I was just coming off maternity-leave from having my son, Chance. I'd given birth at the age of 38 years-old. Which doctors say is old for birthing children. I had also received my license from the California State Board of Cosmetology.

Needless to say, I was blessed and eager to return to work from being out from maternity-leave. I had started to gain a sense of self as a new mom. I was eating great. Sleeping better than I had when my son was first born. All was well in my world. I had my life all mapped out.

My plan was to continue building my clientele and settling into being a new working mom.

Now I was nervous about hiring a nanny or taking my son to daycare, because I felt like he was too small and not speaking well enough to leave with strangers. So naturally, I began to worry.

I asked the Lord what to do. Now this was January 2020, and the mention of there being a virus spreading overseas in China was circulating.

The U.S. president with the orange glow 😊 , was busy making statements that the disease would never reach U.S. soil. Boy was he wrong. Events started to occur rapidly. Kobe Bryant and his daughter had passed away in a fatal plane crash. While the numbers of infected individuals rose higher and higher as the global news reports was delivered on the daily.

Countries were popping up out of the woodworks stating that they were experiencing large outbreaks of COVID in their heavily populated areas. By the time New York reported several cases in their state, California's large metropolitan areas started to see significant numbers of infected cases arise.

Each broadcast of COVID cases rising, heightened my anxieties. I was already trying to adjust to becoming a new mom. Now the outside world was experiencing high infection rates of a new viral infection that was creating mass hysteria all over the world!

I'd become a ball of nerves. My decision making became cloudy. Internally, I couldn't decipher between feelings, fear, and facts. I was a mess. I was suddenly not ready to face the day.

> "What would I do with my son when I returned to work?"

I had just stopped breastfeeding.

> "How would my son adjust to being around a stranger while I picked up where I left off with building my new cosmetology clientele?"

Deep inside my heart I wasn't ready to be apart from my baby for a long period of time. Especially, not the long hours I was used to spending at the beauty salon. This virus was spreading like wildfire. Then there was lupus.

Me living with a preexisting illness that had been sleeping for months before finding out I was pregnant with my son.

What would happen if lupus was awakened by encountering someone who had COVID? Or worse, what if me or the baby contracted COVID?

My first instinct was to go to my **war room** (prayer closet) and petition God for direction. I started asking the Holy Spirit to impart wisdom and order my steps (Psalm 119:133).

> "Dear Lord, how can I build my clientele and continue to develop a close bond with my son? How can I provide for my family and still build my brand? How can I continue to keep lupus at bay and maintain my physical health, while quarantining?

I had so many questions running through my head. I started to hear the Holy Spirit whisper the word **"Pivot"**, repeatedly in my spirit.

When I hear a word from the Lord, my confirmation comes in threes. Soon after receiving that impartation from the Lord, I started to see the word being used all over social media; and even tv programs. As I settled on the word that the Father gave me, I felt a settling in my spirit. Then, I heard the word again.

Pivot!

Suddenly, I started seeing visions and ideas based on my different gifts. God reminded me of my inspirational videos that I'd started making to encourage people living with chronic illnesses and disabilities, back in 2018.

Then there were all the book ideas that I'd been contemplating for the past 10 years that I'd written down. Ideas and titles of various books and journals. Then there was my gifting in the beauty industry.

I had created a hair growth serum to grow my hair back, after chemotherapy treatment in years past. I could see formulas for different hair products and treatments for people dealing with hair loss.

All these ideas were things that I could do. I just needed to prioritize them in order. So once again I went to God.

> *"Lord what do I do first? Because I know if I try to do it in my own power; I will fall short. I will become overwhelmed and not attempt not one thing that was revealed to me. Father God, please help me. Lead and guide me step-by-step. I promise I will follow. Amen."*

All I could hear is, **Pivot!**

Suddenly, a God-moment hit me like a ton of bricks! 🤯 🧱 ‼️ ....

Willie Moore Jr. was advertising a class that his company was offering on the internet. The name of the program was, "Monetize Your Mojo." The price was right. The timing was perfect. And I was ready to go.

As the contents of the course poured into me, I was able to line my projects up, one-by-one. Although my dreams seemed too large and lofty; little by little I worked my way to accomplish each goal. I started with my video blog/podcast.

God had imparted wisdom knowledge in me to present on my social media pages. I worked on my timing and presentation. I researched different scriptures and information that aligned with my message for the week. I created a schedule and stuck to it.

Then came my writing…

I started drafting an outline about my life living with a chronic illness (lupus). Then God stopped me in my tracks. He then charged me with the task of writing this devotional.

I was so scared to write this devotional because I didn't think anyone would want to read about god's grace from little ole' me. However, each time I placed my fingers on the keys of my computer. Or the keyboard on my phone. And then the speak-to-text option. The words poured out of me.

In my insecure moments He assured me with scripture that I was walking in the path that He had designed for me in this season of my life.

Then came my beauty industry dreams. I remembered meeting with a haircare product line specialist in 2019, and I tracked down the notes that I'd written down in the masterclass.

Whenever it was time to start building my hair and skin care product lines, I would have the right information and people to call to bring the product to fruition.

With each idea or desire that came to mind, I was able to write the idea down, pray over it, and submit it to God. I wrote the visions that God had graced me with. And there it was, my outline and roadmap to **Pivot.**

Now it's your turn. I hope that this chapter has ignited a fire in you. A directive that will encourage you to activate your faith. You gotta get ready to Pop that Thang in Jesus name 😊. Let's pray.

Prayer

Dear Heavenly Father, first off; I want to thank You for being an all-knowing God. You sit high and look low. I thank You for the divine word to Pivot. Lord help me to write down and prioritize my gifts that are making room for me in the earth (Proverbs 18:16 NKJV). Give me the courage I need to activate my faith and walk in the path that You have designed for my life. In Your mighty name I pray, Amen!

Exercise

Now is the time for you to zero-in on your Pivot list. Identify the gifts that have been placed inside of you. After you have brought them to the forefront of your mind, go to God and ask Him how you should prioritize your listed items. Lastly, it's time to go to work. You got this! And I can't wait to see what God has placed on the inside of you 😊 !!!

Grace & Gratitude

My Pivot Move(s)

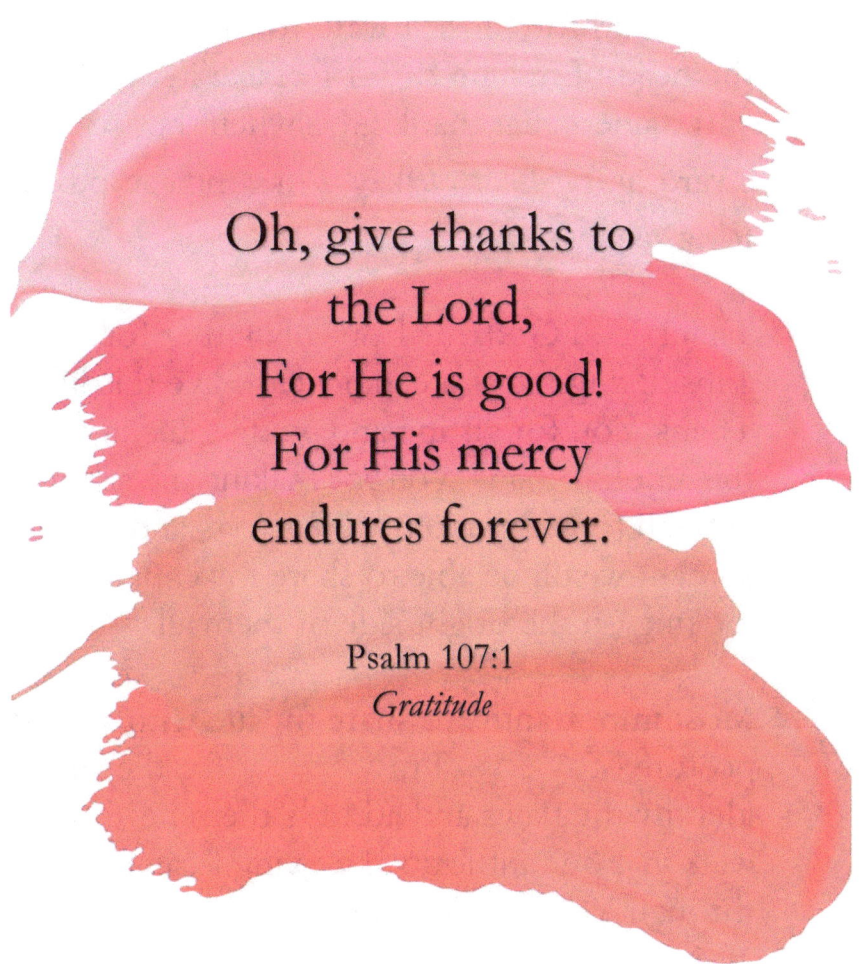

Oh, give thanks to the Lord,
For He is good!
For His mercy endures forever.

Psalm 107:1
Gratitude

My List of Gratitude

"First and foremost, I want to thank God who is the head of my life …" I feel like I sound like the entertainers that thank God when they win an award on tv 😆 ‼️ Okay, I'm gonna stop being silly for a second 😊.

Thank You God, my heavenly father for considering me as a candidate to live this life. Thank You for gifting and guiding me in writing this book. I thank You for making me strong enough to withstand my life's tests and trials, and somehow still be able to share my experiences while looking on the bright side of them all.

Most importantly, to share my life with a heart posture of Grace. I'm Grateful for the ability to identify my flaws and address them head on. To walk in Your authority, knowing I can do all things through Your Power and Grace (Philippians 4:13).

Grace & Gratitude

To my family, y'all were all my first teachers, friends, cheerleaders, confidants, protectors, and providers. Each one of you have encouraged me in ways you don't even understand. Don't worry, that series of books are on their way. 😊

I've watched you all persevere through your tests and trials. Now, seeing y'all win has blessed me to keep going, even when my health tries to snatch my edges. 🤣

I love you all with all that I am. I hope my stories bring up fond memories and make you giggle here and there. Well…. At least the experiences that turned out for the better. 😘

To my friends, colleagues, clients, church families, and associates; y'all give me life. When I started my videos you all would message me or see me in person and say, " I love your messages Charnyce. Don't stop posting."

So, I write this book and each book thereafter as a message of encouragement to you. Thank you.

For those of you who I have yet to meet in person or online, I can't wait to meet and connect with you. 😊

To my son Chance,

Your existence gives me a reason to live past the pains of my life. I wake up each day striving to make your world great!! I can't wait to see what kind of gracious man you become.

Your energy inspires me. I wish I could bottle it up and sell it. We would be billionaires!!! 😉 Ting! Then I would be able to carve out even more playtime with you.

Stay strong little guy and don't stop moving forward. Stay positive and continue to be a gracious kid while drinking your lemon-water and minding your business.

No matter how many "No's'" the world tells you, keep moving forward. You only need one "Yes", and God will do the rest.

Charnyce Everythings New Perdue

Prayer

Lord God, give me the strength to see the good in every relationship in my life. Let my list of Thank You's be a lamp to my feet and a light to my path. Where strength surrounds my heart and fill me with joy and peace. In your name I pray, Amen.

Exercise

Now I want to encourage you to write your list of Thank You's. Come on, don't be shy. Even if you feel like the people who have impacted your life did so in a negative way, I bet once you start writing you'll see the grace and gratitude in each relationship. I dare you to do something different with this list than you would've done before reading this book.

Grace & Gratitude

Thank You List

Grace & Gratitude

God's Grace, Our Gratitude

Charnyce Everythings New Perdue

Scriptures found in this Book:

How to use this Devotional, pg. 5:
Habakkuk 2:2-3; Proverbs 29:18, NKJV.

"Grace", page 19:
Psalm 139; Psalm 119:105-112; 2 Corinthians 12:9

"Gratitude", page 31:
1 Thessalonians 5:18; Psalm 118:24; Colossians 3:15; Psalm 107:1; Matthew 6:2; Psalm 106:1; Colossians 3:2-10

Chapter 1, page 40:
Proverbs 18:24

Chapter 3, page 66:
Hebrews 12:2; Psalm 139; Jeremiah 29:11; Malachi 3:10; Philippians 4:11-13; Habakkuk 2:2-3; Psalm 27:14

Chapter 4, page 77:
Matthew 11:28-30; 2 Corinthians 12:9

Chapter 5, page 85:
Jeremiah 29:11-14

Chapter 6, page. 98:

Luke 22-42

Chapter 7, page 106:
Galatians 5:16; Galatians 16-21; pg. 75 – Galatians 5:22-25

Chapter 8, page 122:
Psalm 61:1-4; Nehemiah 8:10

Chapter 9, page 136:

Psalm 86:13; Matthew 11:28-30; Psalm 27:14; 2 Peter 3:9; 2 Timothy 1:7; Psalm 139; 1 Peter 1:7; Jeremiah 29:11; Romans 8:28

Chapter 10, page 148:
Hab 2:2-3; Proverbs 18:16; Philippians 4:5-7, Romans 12:12; Psalm 27:14; Isaiah 55:8-12

Chapter 11, page 158:
115: Psalm 51:17; Micah 7:19; Isaiah 43:25; Malachi 3:10

Chapter 12, page 176:
1 Peter 5:7

Chapter 13, page 185:

Psalm 139; John 7:39, ESV (English Standard Version); Jeremiah 29:11; John 14:26 ESV

Chapter 14, page 192:
Psalm 22:3

Chapter 15, page 199:
Psalm 118:24; Deuteronomy 28:13; Romans 8:28; Hebrews 13:15; Psalm 121:2; Proverbs 10:22; Ephesians 4:2-3

Chapter 16, page 210:
Proverbs 4:1-2, 4-5, 6-9, 10-27, (NIV) New International Version; Psalm 91

Chapter 17, page 227:
Pg. 159- 2 Corinthians

Chapter 18, page 238:
Matthew 14:22-33; Deuteronomy 31:6; Psalm 51:10-19

Chapter 19, page 268:
Matthew 25:23 NKJV

Chapter 20, page 276:
Matthew 18:20; 1 Corinthians 14:33; Acts 10:28; Romans 2:11-16; Psalm 37:4; Matthew 7:7

Chapter 21, page 287:
Jeremiah 29:11; Psalm 119:13; Proverbs 18:16

Definitions & References

Grace, Definition of Grace at Dictionary.com (Google, 2020) www.Google.com, 2020

Gratitude (/ˈgradə,t (y) o͞od/); noun
> the quality of being thankful; readiness to show appreciation for and to return kindness. Example:
> "She expressed her gratitude to the committee for their support."

Forgiveness
forgiveness, "the release of resentment or anger." The research goes on to state that the action to forgive is to, "stop feeling angry or resentful toward (someone) for an offense, flaw, or mistake." (www.psychologytoday.com , 2020).

Covenant, *"noun"* an agreement. "There was a covenant between them that her name was never to be mentioned." **Similar:** Contract, compact, treaty, pact, accord, deal. Bargain, settlement, concordat protocol, entente agreement, arrangement, understanding, pledge, promise, bond, indenture, guarantee, commitment. *Verb* agree by lease, deed, or another legal contract. Example- "The landlord covenants to repair the property." Similar: pledge, promise, agree, contract.

Pivot, "the action of rotating or turning on one foot while protecting your possession." In this case, you would be protecting the basketball." Dictionary.com; (Google, 2020, www.google.com, 2020.)

Scriptures taken from the New King James Version ™. Copywrite © 1982 by Thomas Nelson, Inc. Used by permission. All rights reserved.

Scriptures taken from The Holy Bible, English Standard Version © 2001 by Crossway, a publishing ministry of good News Publishers, ESV Text Edition: 2016.
All rights reserved.

About the Author

Charnyce Everythings New Perdue is a new author straight out of Southern California, born and raised. A woman with a heart for people and service. Born to a family of entrepreneurs and church goers.

With a license in Cosmetology; a bachelor's degree in psychology and a master's degree in social work & social policy. Charnyce shares her life's experiences in self-awareness, self-development, and self-efficacy throughout her writings. With an emphasis on how to connect and strengthen your mind, body, and spirit; while aligning with God's word.

Growing up in the church and beauty salon fuels her passion for affective communication.
 Now, a proud mother of her son, Chance; Charnyce, aims to assist people in stepping out of survival mode and walking into a life where you can thrive.

Charnyce takes this first book to share how adopting a mindset of grace and gratitude can improve your experience of everyday life. Moving forward no matter what your current circumstance. Equipping people with the knowledge and skills to believe that if God is with you, it doesn't matter what comes against you (Romans 8:28-39).

 "If you don't quit; eventually you will reach God's goal for your life". So be sure you strive to "Pop that Thang in Jesus name!" 😊

www.ingramcontent.com/pod-product-compliance
Lightning Source LLC
Chambersburg PA
CBHW070308230426
43664CB00015B/2670